EVANGELISTIC

Women

A STUDY
OF WOMEN'S
MINISTRIES

D0167638

Pamela STEWART

ISBN: 0-9705764-0-4

Printed in the United States by:
Morris Publishing
3212 East Highway 30
Kearney, NE 68847
1-800-650-7888

Preface

It is my hope that this book will be a help to women in identifying and acknowledging the ministry or ministries wherein they can be the most effective in the church. I have talked to many women who want to do more but don't know what to do or where to begin. They know they have much to give but don't know where to start.

This book cites Bible women who were productive in the work of the church, Scriptures concerning women and their work, examples, personal experiences, and a long list of women's ministries.

As you read this book, I pray you will discover your ministry or ministries and go to work in the church. Or, if you already know your ministry, please help other women find the one in which they can best serve. You will find the fulfillment for which you have been searching. You will be forever changed.

Dedication

To evangelistic women all over the world.

To the women in the church at Council Bluffs, Iowa, where I first started working on this material.

To the women instructors at the Bear Valley Bible Institute of Denver. I love working with you and appreciate your encouragement and support.

To my students in the "Nun" class at the BVBID who helped me put the finishing touches on this material.

To all supporters of the BVBID who make it possible for us to be involved in this work.

To my good friends and co-workers, J.J. and Isabel Turner. Thank you for the opportunity for my husband and me to be involved with you in this great work of teaching and training workers for the kingdom and for encouraging me to finish this book.

To my wonderful children and their families who think I am obsessed with my studying and writing at the computer. Thank you for your patience.

To my handsome husband and friend, Bill, who is the greatest encouragement of all.

Contents

❖ CHAPTER ONE ❖

Evangelistic Women

Evangelistic Women‼ Does this title scare you? No, I haven't gone off the deep end and Yes, I know what the Scriptures say concerning women being in subjection to men: "A woman should learn in quietness and full submission. I do not permit a woman to teach or to have authority over a man; she must be silent" (1 Timothy 2:11,12). "Now I want you to realize that the head of every man is Christ, and the head of the woman is man, and the head of Christ is God" (1 Corinthians 11:3). Because of these Scriptures, and others like them, some women feel they can slide along on their husband's coattails, not having much responsibility in the church. They use these Scriptures as an excuse not to become involved in the church and its work. They like it this way because it's easy. Other women say they want to be involved but men get to do all the work in the church. They claim they are suppressed. These women spend too much time worrying about what they can't do, and overlook the many ministries they are authorized to do. Other women truly want to be involved, but don't know where or how. They realize they have many talents and much to contribute, but because of the controversy on the subject they are not sure what to do or where to start.

Women are an important part of the church, the body of Christ. Like men, we are added to the church by the Lord when we obey the gospel: "...the Lord added to their number daily those who were being saved" (Acts 2:47). "...more and more men and women believed in the Lord and were added to their number" (Acts 5:14). God has placed us in the body as He sees fit. He has given us different roles, but equal work. We are all important, whether we are rich or poor, educated or unlearned, male or female:

> Now the body is not made up of one part but of many. If the foot should say, "Because I am not a hand, I do not belong to the body," it would not for that reason cease to be part of the body. And if the ear should say, "Because I am not an eye, I do not belong to the body," it would not for that reason cease to be part of the body. If the whole body were an eye, where would the sense of hearing be? If the whole body were an ear, where would the sense of smell be? But in fact God has arranged the parts in the body, every one of them, just as he wanted them to be (1 Cor. 12:14-18).

God does not expect women to be just pretty ornaments sitting in the pews. He has much work for us to do. To whom did Jesus first appear after His resurrection? Who were the first people who were allowed to proclaim to the disciples that Jesus had risen from the dead? It was women—Mary Magdalene and the other Mary—who had the honor. They were told to do this both by an angel and by Jesus. Can you imagine the excitement in their voices as they first proclaimed that Jesus was alive again? We need to proclaim the Lord's resurrection with just as much excitement today:

> After the Sabbath, at dawn on the first day of the week, Mary Magdalene and the other Mary went to look at the tomb.
>
> There was a violent earthquake, for an angel of the Lord came down from heaven and, going to the tomb, rolled back the stone and sat on it. His appearance was like lightning, and his clothes were white as snow. The guards were so afraid of him that they shook and became like dead men.
>
> The angel said to the women, "Do not be afraid, for I know that you are looking for Jesus, who was crucified. He is not here; He has risen, just as He said. Come see the place where He lay. Then go quickly and tell His disciples: 'He has risen from the dead and is going ahead of you into Galilee. There you will see Him.' Now I have told you."
>
> So the women hurried away from the tomb, afraid yet filled with joy, and ran to tell His disciples. Suddenly Jesus met them. "Greetings," he said. They came to Him, clasped His feet and worshipped Him. Then Jesus said to them, "Do not be afraid. Go and tell my brothers to go to Galilee; there they will see me" (Matthew 28:1-10).

God gave women the responsibility of managing the home: "So I counsel younger widows to marry, to have children, to manage their homes and to give the enemy no opportunity for slander" (1 Tim. 5:14). If we do it right, managing the home is an enormous responsibility. Yes, and God gave this responsibility to women. I have known people who were surprised to find God put this much trust in women.

Women are told to teach and train other women: "...teach the older women to be reverent in the way they live, not to be slanderers or addicted to much wine, but to teach what is good. Then they can train the younger women to love their husbands and children, to be self-controlled and pure, to be busy at home, to be kind, and to be subject to their husbands, so that no one will malign the word of God" (Titus 2:3-5).

Women, along with men, are called to be Christ's ambassadors: "We are therefore Christ's ambassadors, as though God were making His appeal through us..." (2 Cor. 5:20). We are familiar with ambassadors for the United States representing our country to other countries. As Christ's ambassadors we represent Him to people with whom we come in contact.

Several Scriptures inform us that the church actually met in the homes of women: "Give my greetings to the brothers at Laodicea, and to Nympha and the church in her house" (Colossians 4:15). "Then Peter came to himself and said, 'Now I know without a doubt that the Lord sent His angel and rescued me from Herod's clutches and from everything the Jewish people were anticipating.' When this had dawned on him, he went to the house of Mary the mother of John, also called Mark, where people had gathered and were praying" (Acts 12:11,12).

We also know that women helped support Jesus and His apostles monetarily:

> After this, Jesus traveled about from one city and village to another, proclaiming the good news of the kingdom of God. The Twelve were with Him, and also some women who had been cured of evil spirits and diseases; Mary, called Magdalene, from whom seven demons had come out; Joanna the wife of Cuza, the

manager of Herod's household; Susanna; and many
others. These women were helping to support them out
of their own means (Luke 8:1-3).

Many other women are mentioned in the Scriptures.
Phoebe is said to be a servant of the church and a
great help to many: "I commend to you our sister
Phoebe, a servant of the church in Cenchreae. I ask
you to receive her in the Lord in a way worthy of the
saints and to give her any help she may need from
you, for she has been a great help to many including
me" (Romans 16:1,2). Priscilla was a woman who
traveled with her husband and Paul on one of the
missionary journeys: "Greet Priscilla and Aquila, my
fellow workers in Christ Jesus. They risked their lives
for me. Not only I but all the churches of the Gentiles
are grateful to them. Greet also the church that meets
at their house..." (Rom. 16:3,4). Mary, Tryphaena,
Tryphosa, and Persis are women who Paul says work
very hard for the Lord: "Greet Mary, who worked very
hard for you... Greet Tryphena and Tryphosa, those
women who worked hard in the Lord. Greet my dear
friend Persis, another woman who has worked very
hard in the Lord" (Rom. 16:6,12).

From these examples we can see that women are
very important to God. Although He has not called us
to lead the church or to usurp authority over men, He
has called us to many great works. The works we are
called to do are not less important than those He has
called men to do.

Women will be more effective in the work we are
called to do if we will identify and acknowledge the
ministry or ministries where we have interests and
talents, and where we can be the most effective in the
kingdom. Look over the many ministries listed in this

book and decide in which one you can be the most effective. Then acknowledge your decision to the other women in your Bible study group (your sisters in Christ) and to your eldership (the men who shepherd your congregation).

What is the purpose of identifying and acknowledging our ministries? Women need to feel good about their work, to feel worthwhile to the body, to feel appreciated and accepted. Dr. James Dobson, in his book *What Wives Wish Husbands Knew About Women*, listed a low self-esteem as one of women's greatest problems. This method of identifying and acknowledging could go a long way toward helping correct the problem in this area. Women will no longer feel suppressed or unaccepted.

We should identify and acknowledge our area of work in order to have an approved plan. Nothing is more frustrating than trying to do a good job for the Lord, and at the same time feeling that perhaps someone does not completely approve. If we present a plan to the elders, and we receive their approval and their blessings, we can go forward with our plan. One woman says the main reason she is not using her talents in the church is because she does not know what is acceptable and what is not in terms of women's work. Because she does not want to cause a problem, she does not work to her potential. Her beautiful talents and vibrant energies are wasted on secular clubs and programs. We cannot accomplish anything without a plan. As one of my students said in class, "You can't get there if you don't know where you're going."

We should identify and acknowledge our area of work in order to be dependable women, and to take our work seriously. It should not be a hit or miss work that we do if and when we feel like it. We should be responsible and accountable. If we are dependable, it will take a burden off the leaders of our congregation, because they will know that particular work is being done. They can put their time and effort in another direction.

We should identify and acknowledge our ministry or ministries in the church in order to be more focused. Multi-talented women have a tendency to dabble in many things and not be complete or successful at any. By being focused we can set our priorities. This will allow us to enjoy our ministry, and not feel guilty when we can't be involved in everything.

God expects us to use the talents He has blessed us with. We can see from one of Jesus' parables that he is displeased with us if we are lazy:

> The man who had received the five talents brought the other five. "Master," he said, "you entrusted me with five talents. See, I have gained five more."
>
> His Master replied, "Well done, good and faithful servant! You have been faithful with a few things; I will put you in charge of many things. Come and share your master's happiness."
>
> The man with the two talents also came. "Master," he said, "you entrusted me with two talents; see, I have gained two more."
>
> His Master replied, "Well done, good and faithful servant! You have been faithful with a few things; I will put you in charge of many things. Come and share your master's happiness!"
>
> Then the man who had received the one talent came. "Master," he said, "I knew that you are a hard man, harvesting where you have not sown and gathering

where you have not scattered seed. So I was afraid and went out and hid your talent in the ground. See here is what belongs to you."

His master replied, "You wicked, lazy servant! So you knew that I harvested where I have not sown and gather where I have not scattered seed? Well then, you should have put my money on deposit with the bankers, so that when I returned I would have received it back with interest.

"Take the talent from him and give it to the one who has the ten talents. For everyone who has will be given more, and he will have an abundance. Whoever does not have, even what he has will be taken from him" (Matt. 25:20-29).

When we use our talents, He gives us more. I know this is true because I have seen it happen in my own life. I've also known women who said they had no talents who started to work in the church in some small way and discovered talents they didn't know they had. The opposite is also true. If we fail to use our talents, or to develop potential talents, we are wasting great blessings.

All things are to be done from a heart of love. None of our ministries will be effective if love is not present. God will not bless our ministries if we are doing it out of duty or for social gratification. Jesus spoke of love more than anything else. He said it is the identifying mark to tell others that we are truly His disciples. He personally preached it and lived it. He asked us to follow His example: "All men will know you are my disciples if you love one another" (John 13:35). I once did a survey to determine what draws people to the church. About seventy percent said it was relationships with Christians. A Christian friend reached out in love and taught them about Jesus. Without love we are just going through the motions. The wheels are turning, but we are not going anywhere. We are just making noise. We are like a resounding gong or a clanging cymbal:

> If I speak in the tongues of men and of angels, but have not love, I am only a resounding gong or a clanging cymbal. If I have the gift of prophecy and can fathom all mysteries and all knowledge, and if I have a faith that can move mountains, but have not love, I am nothing. If I give all I possess to the poor and surrender my body to the flames, but have not love, I gain nothing (1 Cor. 13:1-3).

What are some of the traits of love that we must develop? Just saying I need to do all things from a heart of love sounds easy. But when we look a little closer at what love means, what is required of us becomes more of a reality:

> Love is patient, love is kind. It does not envy, it does not boast, it is not proud. It is not rude, it is not self-seeking, it is not easily angered, it keeps no record of wrongs. Love does not delight in evil but rejoices in the truth. It always protects, always trusts, always hopes, always perseveres (1 Cor. 13:4-7).

When people come through our doors at church, they are not looking for the truth. They do not know there is a truth. They are looking for a place to belong, a place to feel loved and accepted.

Learning to love is a continual effort. It is something we will never completely conquer. But we have the perfect teacher of love by which to pattern ourselves. To be patient and kind takes practice. Jesus made the ultimate love sacrifice, and He told us that the greatest commandment is to love God and our neighbor:

> "Teacher, which is the greatest commandment in the law?"
>
> Jesus replied; "'Love the Lord your God with all your heart and with all your soul and with all your mind.' This is the first and greatest commandment. And the second is like it: 'Love your neighbor as yourself'" (Matt. 22:36-39).

As we look through the many ministries for women, and as we find Bible examples of women being effective in the church, let us identify and acknowledge our areas of work. It's time for women to decide to get serious about the work God has given us. It's time for women to decide in which areas of work we can be the most effective. It's time for women to be focused and dependable. It's time for women to realize how important we are to God and His church. It's time for women to learn to love the church, its leaders, and its members as God calls us to do.

Discussion Questions

1. Should women be evangelistic? Are you? In what ways?

2. Why are women confused about their work in the church?

3. Give several reasons from this chapter why it is important for women to identify and acknowledge their ministries.

4. Discuss the women named in this chapter. In what ways were they leaders?

5. What does it mean to be an ambassador for Christ?

6. In light of the parable in Matthew 25:20-29, what happens when we use our talents? What happens when we do not use our talents?

7. Are you using your talents in the church? In what ways?

8. Over the years has God given you more talents, or taken away talents? Why?

9. Discuss ministries done out of love versus ministries done out of duty.

10. What are people looking for when they visit the church?

— NOTES —

❖ CHAPTER TWO ❖

Power for Effective Ministries

Many times we do not realize the vast amount of power we have as children of God. Sometimes we spend so much time teaching obedience to the gospel that we forget to emphasize the privileges that come with obeying.

A Christian woman is not an ordinary woman. She is different from women who do not belong to Christ. She has power that ordinary women do not have.

Today it is very important to understand how special it is to be one of God's children, because Christianity sometimes gets a bad rap. Just recently I heard people talking about "those religious people" as if we were the bad guys.

During my lifetime, the majority of the people in my surroundings have been believers in God. When I was a child, the Scriptures were read and a prayer was said at school the first thing every morning. Everyone in my class believed in God. Children no longer hear the Word of God read every day. A large percent are not exposed to it at all. Generations of young people are growing up not believing in God.

We need to be reminded often of the power we possess in Christ in order to stay strong when others ridicule. It is a special privilege to be a Christian.

To take advantage of all the power God has for us we must first be sure we are Christians. All God's great promises are for His children.

Power in Forgiveness

God promises us forgiveness of sins. Have you ever wished you could just start over with your life, and all past mistakes could be erased? When we become Christians that is exactly what happens: "Blessed are they whose offenses have been forgiven, whose sins have been covered. Blessed is the man whose sin the Lord will never count against him" (Rom. 4:7,8). However, consequences of sins can follow us. If we have contracted a disease through sexual promiscuity, the consequence of that sin will not go away. Relationships may have been ruined that cannot be restored. But when we become Christians, those sins are forgiven and covered. In God's eyes, it is as though they never occurred.

A young woman once came to me burdened down by guilt over past sexual sins, although she had now given her life to the Lord. She grieved because she would not be a virgin when she married. I explained to her that technically she was right. She could not take away what had happened. But she found great comfort and strength in knowing that God not only forgives, but also covers and will never count those sins against her. In God's eyes, it is as though they were never committed: "Therefore, there is now no condemnation for those who are in Christ Jesus" (Rom. 8:1).

When we become Christians, we must let go of sinful associations, friendships, and activities. Sometimes we want to hang on to one little corner of the world, one little sin that we don't want to give up. To be free of all condemnation, we must not practice sin: "No one who lives in Him keeps on sinning. No one who continues to (practice) sin has either seen him or known him" (1 John 3:6, parenthesis mine). I have known people who have practiced sin in their lives who say, "Everyone sins and this is my sin." They do not try to get the sin out of their lives. They use such verses as "If we claim to be without sin, we deceive ourselves and the truth is not in us" (1 John 1:8) to rationalize: "Since everyone has sin, I can keep this one." This verse means we have all sinned and we continue to sin as Christians, but this does not give us an excuse to "practice" sin, or have a sin in our life that we are not trying to remove.

How do we get into Christ Jesus to receive this blessing? "...Repent and be baptized, every one of you, in the name of Jesus Christ so that your sins may be forgiven. And you will receive the gift of the Holy Spirit" (Acts 2:38). Baptism is the point in time when we actually make a covenant with our Lord, when we reenact Jesus' death, burial, and resurrection and receive the benefits of His sacrifice for us. Forgiveness of sins is one of the blessings we receive when we obey the gospel. God is so good. Other blessings include the indwelling Holy Spirit and admission into Christ's church (Acts 2:47).

Power from the Indwelling Holy Spirit

When we become Christians, the Father sends His Holy Spirit to indwell us. The human heart actually becomes the home of God. What greater power could we imagine? What higher privilege could we desire? "...you yourselves are God's temple and...God's Spirit lives in you" (1 Cor. 3:16). This means we are not on our own to live the Christian life. Many people try to "be good" outside of Christ, and they can to a certain extent. But the person who has the indwelling Holy Spirit has the capability to put to death the sinful things: "...The sinful mind is hostile to God. It does not submit to God's law, nor can it do so. Those controlled by their sinful nature cannot please God" (Rom. 8:7,8). "...but if by the Spirit you put to death the misdeeds of the body, you will live. Those who are led by the Spirit of God are sons of God" (Rom. 8:13,14). The decision to put sin to death must be made before baptism (repentance), but the power to do so comes from the Holy Spirit that indwells us.

God's Holy Spirit living in us should make a difference in everything we do: the way we act, the places we go, the way we dress, the movies and television programs we watch, and the language we use and listen to.

Sometimes it can be very evident who has the indwelling Spirit and who does not. While sitting in the cafe court at the mall, I was observing women. Two women sitting nearby were using ungodly language and inappropriate jesting. Another woman walked by very scantily and sexually clad. Was it apparent that they were not women of power?

The Holy Spirit affects our lives in many ways. He sanctifies us (2 Thessalonians 2:13), helps us in our weakness (Rom. 8:26,27), and is our counselor (John 14:16,17). He also produces Christian character in us as we grow and mature (Galatians 5:22,23).

The fruit of the Spirit includes:

Love — The Christian grace that works out the whole law. The entire law is summed up in a single command: "...love your neighbor as yourself" (Matt. 19:19). It is clear that God did not intend for us to be selfish people. The Holy Spirit helps us develop a heart of love.

Joy — "You became imitators of us and of the Lord; in spite of severe suffering, you welcomed the message with the joy given by the Holy Spirit" (1 Thess. 1:6). The Holy Spirit gives joy in the Christian life even in the face of adversities.

Peace — "And the peace of God, which transcends all understanding, will guard your hearts and your minds in Christ Jesus" (Philippians 4:7). This peace is so wonderful that it passes all our understanding. How can I have such a deep peace with all that is going on in the world? I don't know. I don't understand. But I have it.

Patience — "And we urge you, brothers, warn those who are idle, encourage the timid, help the weak, be patient with everyone" (1 Thess. 5:14). We are encouraged to warn, encourage, and help, but with patience for everyone.

Kindness — "...and to godliness, brotherly kindness..." (2 Peter 1:7). In a world where people are hurting, a simple act of kindness, a touch, or a smile, means so much.

Goodness — "And do not forget to do good and to share with others, for with such sacrifices God is pleased" (Hebrews 13:16). We often hear the phrase, "She's a good woman." This means that she stands for good and she does good. Unfortunately the world has a warped view of what is good. The good produced in us by the Holy Spirit is true goodness.

Faithfulness — "It gave me great joy to have some brothers come and tell about your faithfulness to the truth and how you continue to live according to the truth" (3 John 3). Faithfulness is endurance to God, to our sisters, and to ourselves.

Gentleness — "Be completely humble and gentle; be patient, bearing with one another in love" (Ephesians 4:2). A gentle voice, a gentle touch are evidences of the Spirit's work.

Self Control — "Likewise, teach the older women to be reverent in the way they live, not to be slanderers or addicted to much wine, but to teach what is good. Then they can train the younger women to love their husbands and children, to be self-controlled and pure, to be busy at home, to be kind, and to be subject to their husbands, so that no one will malign the word of God" (Titus 2:3-5). Have you heard someone who was having an outburst of anger say "she made me so mad, I just couldn't help it"? She may be right if she does not have the Holy Spirit.

Power in the Church

God says that the church is the avenue through which all blessings come. One of the blessings that we receive when we become Christians is membership in Christ's church: "...And the Lord added to their number daily those who were being saved" (Acts 2:47). God promises power will be at work in us *through the church*. This makes it very important for us to understand the church: "His intent was that now, *through the church*, the manifold wisdom of God should be made known..." (Ephesians 3:10, emphasis mine). "...I pray that you, being rooted and established in love, may have power, *together with all the saints*, to grasp how wide and long and high and deep is the love of Christ" (Eph. 3:17,18, emphasis mine). "Now to Him who is able to do immeasurably more than all we ask or imagine, according to His power that is at work within us, to him be glory *in the church* and in Christ Jesus throughout all generations..." (Eph. 3:20, emphasis mine).

Joined together with brothers and sisters in the Lord, we have great power as a body of people. We can accomplish much. I've heard people say they want to be a Christian, but they want nothing to do with the church. This is a contradiction of terms. The power is manifested in the church.

The New Testament Christians seemed to understand the power that comes from being together. Acts 2:42-47 gives us an illustration of their commitment to each other:

1. They devoted themselves to the apostles' teaching.
2. They devoted themselves to fellowship.
3. They devoted themselves to breaking of bread.
4. They devoted themselves to prayer.
5. They were filled with awe.
6. They were together.
7. They had all things in common.
8. They gave to anyone as he had need.
9. They continued to meet together.
10. They ate together.

The power was at work in them. The result of all this togetherness was daily conversions: "...And the Lord added to their number daily those who were being saved" (Acts 2:47). It is the Lord that adds us to His church when we become Christians.

Power Through the Word

God gave us a powerful tool by which to live when He preserved His Word. Written by inspiration, it gives us everything we need to be powerful women of God: "All scripture is God-breathed and is useful for teaching, rebuking, correcting, and training in righteousness, so that the man of God may be thoroughly equipped for every good work" (2 Tim. 3:16,17). The guide we live by is not words of man, but teachings directly from God.

We are encouraged to study the Word daily: "Now the Bereans were of more noble character than the Thessalonians, for they received the message with great eagerness and examined the Scriptures every day to see if what Paul said was true" (Acts 17:11). Sometimes I find it difficult to have the time to do this. I rationalize that I study the Word several times a week at church. Isn't that enough? Is it so important to be "daily" in the Word? One of Jesus' parables helped me to understand the need for daily study. He tells a story of an evil spirit coming out of a man. The evil spirit went about seeking rest and did not find it. So he returned to the man he had left and found that house swept clean and put in order. But one thing was missing. It was unoccupied. So he returned to live there, bringing seven more evil spirits with him (Matt. 12:43-45). From this parable, we can see that we must do more than just clean up our act. We must fill our hearts with God's Word so there will be no room for evil to dwell there. The man in the parable failed to fill up with good things and the evil was able to take over again. With this in mind we can see that we must fill our hearts with good things every day.

Philippians 4:8 gives us a list of things to think about to keep our hearts clean:

1. Whatever is true.
2. Whatever is noble.
3. Whatever is right.
4. Whatever is pure.
5. Whatever is lovely.
6. Whatever is admirable.
7. Whatever is excellent.
8. Whatever is praiseworthy.

Paul, the writer of Philippians, tells us these things are learned and must be practiced (Phil. 4:9). They are not things that will just fall into place without effort on our part.

Power Through Prayer

Another powerful tool given to us is prayer. Prayer is a direct link between God and us: "...The prayer of a righteous man is powerful and effective" (James 5:16). "Do not be anxious about anything, but in everything, by prayer and petition, with thanksgiving, present your requests to God" (Phil. 4:6). The writers of the Word stressed the power of prayer. They remembered the saints in their prayers (Eph. 1:16-18; Phil. 1:3). They asked for prayers of the saints for themselves (Eph. 6:19). They encouraged the saints to pray (Eph. 6:18; James 5:13). Jesus taught the disciples to pray (Matt. 6:5-13). He also prayed to the Father for Himself when He faced His death (Matt. 26:39). He prayed for His disciples (Luke 22:31,32). He prayed for children (Matt. 19:13-15).

Developing a daily prayer life is crucial. We will never feel close to God until we learn to talk to Him. I have known women who keep a prayer journal. This allows them to be focused as they write words of praise, thanksgiving, and requests. Later they can look back and see how God answered their prayers.

I am amazed at what God does through the prayers of the saints. In my personal life, I have proved His power through prayer over and over. If I am having trouble delivering a lesson or concentrating when I'm writing, I stop and think, "I am trying to do this on my own power. I haven't prayed." Things are much different after I pray. If I am having difficulty overcoming a sin, I stop and think, "I am trying to overcome this on my own power." Prayer has changed many things in my life. The strange thing is that I am always amazed. I know Jesus promised answered prayers, but I continually stand in awe when I see them answered.

With all this power—being a child of God, forgiveness of sins, God dwelling in us, the fellowship of the believers, and the power of prayer—we have much help to lead a life for Christ and to be thoroughly equipped for ministry.

Discussion Questions

1. List five areas of power God has given to help us lead the Christian life and to help us be effective in our ministries.

2. List ways each has helped you in your life.

3. Who are the people whose sins are covered?

4. Where does God's Holy Spirit dwell?

5. List and discuss the fruit of the Spirit.

6. Where is the manifold wisdom of God made known?

7. List ways in which members of the New Testament church were committed to each other.

8. Why is it important to study the Word every day? (Discuss the parable in the text.)

9. List reasons we sometimes do not study every day.

10. List the benefits of keeping a prayer journal.

— NOTES —

❖ CHAPTER THREE ❖

What Hinders Our Ministry?

Many times women strive to be effective in their ministries but with no success. They are going through the motions but there is no fruit, no harvest. The truth is that only when we completely give ourselves to the Lord can we be effective in reaching others through any ministry.

When I ask women why we don't talk about the Lord, I usually get answers such as fear of being rejected, fear of sounding stupid, and fear of not knowing enough about the Bible to give a correct answer. These are superficial excuses. We must look for a deeper reason.

A Misunderstanding of the Holy Spirit's Power Hinders

One of the greatest hindrances to our ministries is denying that we have the great Power of God, His Holy Spirit, indwelling us: "having a form of godliness, but denying its power..." (2 Tim. 3:5). The Holy Spirit cannot be effective if we deny that He exists within us. I find many women who intellectually know the power is there but deny it by not relying on it. This makes God seem far away and impersonal. People who deny the power are the ones who have trouble putting to death the sinful deeds of the body. They continually fight the same sins all their lives. These sins can be denounced through the power of the Holy Spirit.

Do you know someone like this? Someone who has been a weak Christian all his or her life, never able to be a good influence for the Lord, or to be effective in the church. Jamie became a Christian very early in life. At first she was eager to learn but she had many problems. She struggled to be faithful. She struggled with sin. You often found her on the front seat when the invitation song was sung at church. She would declare her desire to try harder and do better, and she would be for periods of time. Jamie was denying the power. She was trying to "be good" on her own steam and not on God's.

We hinder our ministries when we suppress the Spirit: "Do not put out the Spirit's fire" (1 Thes. 5:19). Another version uses the word 'quench.' The word 'quench' means to suppress or put out the Spirit's fire. The people who do this know the Spirit lives within them, but the Spirit does not affect them because they keep Him suppressed.

We can hinder our ministries by grieving the Spirit: "And do not grieve the Holy Spirit of God, with whom you were sealed for the day of redemption. Get rid of all bitterness, rage and anger, brawling and slander, along with every form of malice. Be kind and compassionate to one another, forgiving each other, just as in Christ God forgave you" (Eph. 4:30-32). It's a sad picture to think of the Holy Spirit grieving because of our actions, yet that is exactly what happens. When we grieve the Holy Spirit living within us, this can affect us spiritually, physically, and emotionally. Has there been a time in your life when you were grieving? Maybe you had lost a loved one to death, or had a great disappointment in your job, or a friend had let you down. Remember what it feels like to grieve? Were you effective in your ministries at this time in your life? No, you were not effective at much of anything. You just got by from one day to another. Your concerns and thoughts had turned to yourself. When the Spirit is grieving because of our sinfulness, He can't be effective either. He cannot work in our lives. Let's admit we have the great power of God living in us. Let's depend on Him and call on Him to help us be effective in our ministries: "...The world cannot accept this Counselor, because it neither sees him nor knows him. But you know him, for he lives with you and will be in you" (John 14:17).

Unrepented Sin Hinders

Unrepented sin is probably one of the greatest hindrances to our ministries. Our lack of effectiveness can come from an unrepentant heart. Is there a sin that I am not willing to give up for the Lord? The Holy Spirit can't live in a body that continually practices a sin, one that is controlled by the sinful nature: "If we deliberately keep on sinning after we have received the knowledge of the truth, no sacrifice for sins is left, but only a fearful expectation of judgment and of raging fire that will consume the enemies of God" (Heb. 10:26,27). Sometimes it is hard to harmonize the marvelous grace God extends to us, who live by the Spirit but sin out of weakness, with a person who is controlled by the sinful nature. When we occasionally sin, we are not practicing sin and God's grace continually covers us: "...if we walk in the light, as he is in the light, we have fellowship with one another, and the blood of Jesus, his Son, purifies us from every sin" (1 John 1:7). However, if we are controlled by the sinful nature and our attitude is that God's grace will cover whatever we do, we are in trouble: "No one who lives in him keeps on sinning. No one who continues to sin has either seen him or known him" (1 John 3:6).

David's story in Psalms 51 gives us a picture of a contrite sinner's prayer for pardon. Verse seven says "cleanse me." Verse nine says "blot out all my iniquities." Verse 10 says "create in me a clean heart and renew a steadfast spirit within me." Verse 11 says "Do not cast me from your presence or take your Holy Spirit from me." Verse 12 says "restore to me the joy of your salvation." Verse 13 says "Then I will teach transgressors your ways; and sinners will turn back to you." Notice after we have repented, are cleansed, and are restored, joy is restored. Then we will teach others. Then we can be effective in our ministries. Unrepented sin can pull us down and burden us. It robs us of our joy. When we are burdened and without joy, it isn't likely that we will try to share the gospel with anyone.

Such was the case with Deb. She had held on to a sin for years. Other Christians told her that grace would cover it. She tried to convince herself that everyone had some sin in their lives and this was hers. She knew it would be difficult to get rid of this addiction and she really enjoyed having it. She had no joy, no peace, and she was not effective in her ministries. Eventually, she was called to repentance. Someone came along and said, "According to the Scripture, you are committing a willful sin. You won't go to heaven unless you repent." The stern call to repentance from God's Word worked.

She gave it up. Her joy was restored and she is now effective in her ministries.

Timidity Hinders

Timidity hinders our ministries. Many women feel they are too timid to speak up for the Lord. This does not come from God. The Scripture says: "For God did not give us a spirit of timidity, but a spirit of power, of love, and of self-discipline" (2 Tim. 1:7). If timidity does not come from God, who does it come from? It comes from the devil. The devil is very happy when we hold back and are afraid to speak out about the Lord.

Guilt Hinders

Guilt follows closely behind these other hindrances in being a stealer of our effectiveness. God forgave us, but we can't seem to forgive ourselves. The Bible gives us many examples of people of God who were involved in sin whom He forgave. David was said to be a man after God's own heart, yet he was involved in sin with Bethsheba. God forgave him. Sarah doubted God when He told her she would have a child in her old age. God forgave her. The more we study the Bible, the more we will see that we are not alone in being sinners. Paul gives us the answer: "...But one thing I do: Forgetting what is behind and straining toward what is ahead, I press on toward the goal to win the prize for which God has called me heavenward in Christ Jesus" (Phil. 3:13,14).

Worldliness Hinders

Worldliness is a hindrance to our ministries. Those people who teach Bible class on Sunday morning but use inappropriate language and jesting through the week haven't really given over to the Lord. Television has made things that are wrong seem normal. We have become insensitive to worldliness. A worldly person can't be effective in the kingdom. In fact, the Bible tells us these people are enemies of the cross: "For, as I have often told you before and now say again even with tears, many live as enemies of the cross of Christ. Their destiny is destruction, their god is their stomach, and their glory is in their shame. Their mind is on earthly things" (Phil. 3:18,19). Having our minds on earthly, worldly things is a definite distraction from our ministries. We all must have a job, but our jobs are not the most important things in our lives. They are only a means to provide for our families. They should not rule us. Hobbies are fun. Entertainment is relaxing. But in eternity it won't matter if we had a great job, made a lot of money, were an excellent golfer, or loved to watch television. While all these are fine, an excess of them could be debauchery and could be getting in our way of serving the Lord. Our priorities should be on eternal things. Our involvement in earthly things such as jobs and hobbies can be used for eternal significance by remembering our purpose at all times: "Since, then, you have been raised with Christ, set your hearts on things above, where Christ is seated at the right hand of God. Set your minds on things above, not on earthly things. For you died, and your life is now hidden with Christ in God" (Col. 3:1-3).

Attitudes Hinder

Many times Christians do not understand God's wonderful grace and what it means in our lives now and in eternity. They go through life without the radiant joy that was meant for us. They fuss and worry when troubles come just as the world does. They are not content and it shows in their faces and body language. God meant for us to be joyous people even in the midst of trials. The best way to have joy is to understand His grace. An understanding of grace will lead us to the peace we desire, but is beyond our understanding: "Do not be anxious about anything, but in everything, by prayer and petition, with thanksgiving, present your requests to God. And the peace of God, which transcends all understanding, will guard your hearts and your minds in Christ Jesus" (Phil. 4:6,7). The book of Philippians is the "joy" book of the Bible. If Paul had been in perfect circumstances when he wrote the book we would say, "I could be joyous also if everything were perfect in my life." But Paul was far from being in perfect circumstances. He was in prison and did not know if he would live or die. His work of preaching and teaching as he traveled around the country had been interrupted when he was arrested. Yet, sixteen times in this book he mentions joy, rejoice, or be glad. He is trying to tell us what we have in Christ surpasses all the things that go on in the world. You may say, "I want this joy, this peace." It is a fruit of the Spirit and will come as we mature in Christ. Our old nature says be unhappy, let troubles get you down. The devil loves us that way because we can't be effective. The Spirit within us says be joyous, I have great things planned for you.

Worry Hinders

It is difficult to get to a maturity in our spiritual lives when we can honestly say we do not worry. All of us who have raised children know there has been plenty to worry about. But worry stifles us, robs us of our joy, and gives us all kinds of physical problems as well. We must learn to depend on God, and believe Him when He says, "All things work together for good for those that love the Lord" (Romans 8:28). As we meditate on His Word and walk with Him, we draw closer to the peace he offers. Jesus reminds us that He feeds the birds and He tells us we are more important than birds. He tells us He clothes the beautiful lilies of the field, which only last a short time, and He says He will clothe us also. He tells us that pagans are the ones who worry about these things, not us, and He says if we seek His kingdom first, everything else will be given to us (Matt. 6:25-34).

Excuses Hinder

The excuses we make to ourselves and to God hinder our ministries. We rationalize to the point that we can fool ourselves into thinking our excuses are good. We make excuses out of weakness of our mind and body. Christ will give us wisdom and strength to overcome if we ask Him.

We are not the inventor of excuses. People of God in Biblical times were just as guilty. When God told Moses he had chosen him to lead His people out of Egypt, Moses made many excuses as to why he could not. Ultimately God's will was accomplished, but not without resistance from Moses. Look at the paraphrased dialogue between God and Moses in Exodus 3 and 4.

God: "I am sending you to Pharaoh to bring my people the Israelites out of Egypt."

Moses: "Who am I, that I should go?"

God: "I will be with you."

Moses: "Suppose I go to the Israelites and tell them you sent me and they ask who you are?"

God: "Tell them 'I AM.'"

Moses: "What if they won't listen and don't believe me?"

God: "I'll give you evidences."

Moses: "I have never been eloquent. I am slow of speech and tongue."

God: "Who gave man his mouth? I will help you speak and teach you what to say."

Moses: "Oh Lord, please send someone else."

God: "I am angry. Get your brother Aaron. I will help both of you speak, and will teach you what to do."

God's purpose was accomplished. God will work out His will through His people. We cannot fight against Him. He always wins. We might as well stop making excuses. They will be of no use in the long run. We will only delay the work God has for us. Now why is it that you have not approached your neighbor for a Bible study?

Not long ago a woman called, asking for help with a problem. At first she said she had a friend with this problem. Her question was, "What would you tell someone who knows she should read the Bible and pray every day, but she isn't getting anything out of it? When she reads, she is just calling words. And when she prays, it doesn't feel as though the prayers are getting any higher than the ceiling. Sometimes she falls asleep trying to pray. She is not being effective in her ministries." I said, "Well, let's take an inventory. Is this person a Christian?" Yes, she had obeyed the Gospel.

"So, what is hindering God's work in her life?" We went down the list. Is she denying the Holy Spirit's power? Is she quenching or grieving the power? Are there sins she won't give up for God? Is there timidity, guilt, worldliness, or an attitude problem? Is she worrying and making excuses? Is her joy gone because of these things? She listened. Then she began to cry. I asked if she was close enough to her friend to talk to her about these things, or would the friend be offended. She said "No, the person is not offended. The person is me, and you have helped me so very much." I never knew what was the cause of her problem, but somewhere in the list she found the cause. She knew. There was a tremendous difference in her after that. She said she took the list of things that could be hindering her and did an inventory on herself. She asked God for help. Her joy was restored. She was able to read her Bible, pray, and share with others. She was able to see and discard the hindrances.

Let each one of us do an inventory on ourselves and lay aside what is holding us back: "Therefore, since we are surrounded by such a great cloud of witnesses, let us throw off everything that hinders and the sin that so easily entangles, and let us run with perseverance the race marked out for us" (Heb. 12:1).

Discussion Questions

1. Why do some people deny the Power of the Holy Spirit? What effect does this have?

2. Are you quenching the Holy Spirit? How can you stop?

3. Is there an unrepented sin in your life that hinders your ministry and your Christian walk?

4. Discuss a time when you grieved. How did you feel? Does this help you understand how the Spirit feels when He is grieving?

5. Where does timidity come from?

6. Discuss how guilt and worldliness hinder.

7. Does your joy show to others? How can you improve on this?

8. Do you have the peace that Paul talks about in Philippians? If not, how can you get it?

9. Do an inventory alone—or with a sister—to determine if anything is hindering your ministry.

10. Discuss Hebrews 12:1.

— NOTES —

❖ CHAPTER FOUR ❖

Women in Family Ministries

Whatever ministry we choose in our work for the Lord, there is one that all married women with children have in common. It is a ministry that requires daily attention and should never be neglected. The Bible exhorts women to marry, have children, and manage their homes: "So I counsel younger widows to marry, to have children, to manage their homes and to give the enemy no opportunity for slander" (1 Tim. 5:14). If we have a family, this is our most important ministry.

God never intended for Christian women to neglect their homes, husbands, and children in order to go out and work for Him. When we are caring for, teaching, and training our children, we are working for Him. When we are being helpers to our husbands and striving to build strong Christian marriages, we are working for Him. Women should not neglect their first ministry to advance another.

There is no greater ministry than being Christian helpers for our husbands: "The Lord God said, 'It is not good for the man to be alone. I will make a helper suitable for him'" (Genesis 2:18). Are you suitable for your husband? When my husband and I were married, I had no idea what a suitable mate for him meant. Nor did he know what I needed. We only knew we were in love and wanted to spend the rest of our lives together. Knowing each other's needs and how to fulfill them is not an automatic process as many people think. It takes effort. Why? Because men and women are very different. If I try to figure my husband out based on my feelings and my emotions, I am in trouble. He does not think as I do. As we grew and matured together, we each learned and continue to learn what the other needs. It is a lifetime process, and one that takes work. I am thankful for the many good books and tapes available to us today.

To have a successful marriage, both the husband and wife must be Christians. They must be dedicated to God. They must want to have a good marriage to please Him, as well as each other. Most marriages are not strong enough to resist the temptations of this world based only on their love for each other. There must be a higher power at work here also. To have the same Christian value system is a tremendous help. For instance, my husband and I knew when we got married that divorce was not an option. Whatever came, we knew we would always be together. Knowing that has helped us work through many problems.

Good communication in a marriage is the next most important thing. This involves so many aspects. It involves talking and listening. It involves respecting each other's opinions, whether or not you agree with them. It involves not having an angry outburst even if you are very angry. It involves talking about intimate things, so you can understand your mate's needs and he can understand yours. Some people are married for years before they find out their mate would like for them to be involved with them in a particular activity. They never talked about it so they never knew. Why don't married people talk? I don't know the answer. Sometimes, when my husband and I are having dinner alone at a restaurant, we try to pick out the couples who are married and those who are not, by their actions and body language. We have seen some couples eat their complete meal without saying a word. We decided they were married.

The best instructions on being good helpers for our husbands are found in Proverbs 31:10-31:

> A wife of noble character who can find?
>
> She is worth far more than rubies. Her husband has full confidence in her and lacks nothing of value. She brings him good, not harm, all the days of her life. She selects wool and flax and works with eager hands. She is like the merchant ships, bringing her food from afar. She gets up while it is still dark; she provides food for her family and portions for her servant girls. She considers a field and buys it; out of her earnings she plants a vineyard. She sets about her work vigorously; her arms are strong for her tasks. She sees that her trading is profitable, and her lamp does not go out at night. In her hand she holds the distaff and grasps the spindle with her fingers. She opens her arms to the poor and extends her hands to the needy. When it snows, she has no fear for her household; for all of them are clothed in scarlet. She makes coverings for her bed; she is clothed in fine linen and purple.
>
> Her husband is respected at the city gate, where he takes his seat among the elders of the land.

> She makes linen garments and sells them, and supplies the merchants with sashes.
>
> She is clothed with strength and dignity; she can laugh at the days to come. She speaks with wisdom, and faithful instruction is on her tongue.
>
> She watches over the affairs of her household and does not eat the bread of idleness.
>
> Her children arise and call her blessed; her husband also, and he praises her;
>
> Many women do noble things, but you surpass them all.
>
> Charm is deceptive, and beauty is fleeting; but a woman who fears the Lord is to be praised. Give her the reward she has earned, and let her works bring her praise at the city gate.

This woman in Proverbs is truly a woman of great value to her husband. Her husband trusts her and has confidence in her. He is respected because she is a good wife. She has never done anything to bring him shame. She is a hard worker both inside and outside the home. She serves her family with food and clothing that she makes. She manages the affairs of her household well. She cares for the poor. She has a home-based business of making and selling linen garments. She fears the Lord. We can learn many good lessons from the woman in this proverb.

There is also no greater ministry than raising Christian children. In the world, nothing much is considered wrong anymore. Children are allowed to watch what they want on television and at the movies. Even some children's movies aren't acceptable. Children aren't taught to respect authority of any kind. Children aren't held accountable for their actions and given consequences to correct them. Too many strong, dedicated women have lost their children to worldliness by not being there to teach these things correctly. They have lost their children while gaining others. What heartache!

Raising our children as God would have us do is one of the biggest jobs we will ever face. In days past, when our efforts were reinforced at school and in the community, our job was easier. The teachers at school read from the Bible and prayed at the beginning of each day. Morality was based on Christian principles from the Bible. This is not the case any longer. We do not have a network of helpers at school. Bible-based morality has long been removed from schools. We hear the government and the media trying to figure out why children are involved in drugs, sex, and violence. Can't they see the decline in morality that has steadily occurred since Bible reading and prayer were removed? Hopefully we have a strong support system in our church. But the bottom line is "it is our responsibility." Our homes must provide the environment for the growth we desire for our children.

One of the best Bible examples of a mother and grandmother raising a young man to be a great worker in the kingdom is the story of Eunice, Lois, and Timothy. Paul says Timothy had great faith, which was lived before him and taught to him by his mother and grandmother: "I have been reminded of your sincere faith, which first lived in your grandmother Lois and in your mother Eunice, and I am persuaded, now lives in you also" (2 Timothy 1:5). Timothy had the privilege of traveling with Paul on one of his missionary journeys. Paul spoke highly of him. He called him "...my true son in the faith" (1 Tim. 1:2). Many people were led to the Lord by him. Are you raising a Timothy? Let's raise our children to be active workers in the kingdom. Let's encourage them to be preachers, Bible teachers, and missionaries.

I'm proud to say that I know Christian women today who have become very conscious about their job of training their children. They have gone back to the Bible for instruction. Some are homeschooling in order to provide a more appropriate atmosphere to teach their children; they are using biblical principles as opposed to the worldly principles used in the public schools. They could not care less if their children are popular, or if they wear the latest fashions. In fact, they would rather they not have that peer pressure. If you ask them if they feel their children are missing out on something, they are quick to say, "Yes, that's the idea." I admire and support these women. Of course, it is not always necessary to homeschool. It depends on the schools in your town. Many communities have great Christian schools. Some public schools continue to provide an atmosphere suitable for our children. But don't take it for granted. Go check it out. Keep your eyes and ears open. Our children spend six or seven hours out of each day at school. Let's be sure it is a suitable atmosphere.

Raising Christian children begins before the children are born. A husband and wife dedicate their lives to each other and to the Lord. They are involved in prayer, Bible study, and going to church together. They are setting an environment in which to bring a new life, an environment that will produce a son or daughter who will love the Lord also.

We must teach the children with words and examples. Children are very smart. Our actions must line up with our words. Otherwise we will confuse our children. They will lose respect for us. If we teach our children to tell the truth and they hear us lying about missing work because we were sick when we were not, they catch on fast. They know we are not living what we are saying. It will appear unimportant. Loving and forgiving are better than saying we should love and forgive. If our children see us doing these things, they will do them also. Michael and Debi Pearl, in their book *To Train Up A Child*, make the following statements:

> When the child is young, the parents are the only 'god' he knows. As he awakens to Divine realities, it is through his earthly father that he understands his heavenly Father. Fathers (and mothers also), you are the window through which your young child understands God. A child learns of the character of God through observing the parents. The parents do not have to be perfect, they just need to represent a balance of God's personality. All that God is in infiniteness, the parents should display in the finite. The parents need not be all-powerful, just the child's source of strength. The parents do not have to be all wise, just wise enough to guide the child and warrant admiration. The parents need not be sinless, just demonstrate a commitment to the good and holy. As the child sees the parents' humble dependence on and love for God, because he loves and respects his parents, he will love and honor the one the parents love (33).

We must talk about the Lord in our daily conversations, not just at Bible study time. We must apply His word to our everyday life. Prayers at mealtime and bedtime are not enough. The Scriptures have this to say:

> Love the Lord your God with all your heart and with all your soul and with all your strength. These commandments that I give you today are to be upon your hearts. Impress them on your children. Talk about

> them when you sit at home and when you walk along
> the road, when you lie down and when you get up. Tie
> them as symbols on your hands and bind them on your
> foreheads. Write them on the doorframes of your houses
> and on your gates (Deuteronomy 6:5-9).

We must not think that taking our children to church is giving them a spiritual education. The majority of the teaching must be done at home on a daily basis. I've known some parents who have Scriptures posted all over the house. It reminds me of Old Testament times when they wrote them on the doorframes and the gates. It is a command for us to train our children in the Lord: "Train a child in the way he should go, and when he is old he will not turn from it" (Prov. 22:6). Training takes time and in our busy society many mothers say they do not have the time. It involves making the rules clear and following up to see if the rules are obeyed. It involves discipline when they are not obeyed. It involves consistency.

Have a set time of the day for the family to be together. This is one of my fondest memories of my children's young years. The family may have been scattered in every direction, but at mealtime we all came together. We prayed and then ate together. We talked about the day and each person's experiences. What stories we heard! Then, my husband would read a story from the Bible storybook. The children would listen attentively because they knew he would ask questions after the story was finished. There was always a lesson for today in the story, and we discussed how to apply it to our lives. I have one regret I would like to share with you to prevent you from making the same mistake. Our grown children tell me they resented the phone interruptions during family times. My husband is a preacher, and we felt we had to answer the phone every time it rang. As hard as we tried, we could not always make the call short. Now that we have answering machines, my advice to you is to turn yours on. When your time with your family is completed, you can listen to your messages. This time is too precious and too important to be interrupted. If I could do it over, I would spend more time in my family ministry.

In a home where husband and children are first priorities, children begin to understand who they are and hopefully won't have to search for that all their lives. They learn to relate to others in Godly ways, and those are the ways they will take into their adult world. They begin to understand their real purpose in life as a child of God. If children do not learn these things in a Christian home environment, they will get a warped view out in the world as it is today.

Although we can consider our family our ministry, and it requires much of our time, we don't want to use our children as excuses to keep us from being involved in other ministries that we have God-given talents to do. Choose one that the children can be involved in also, such as the ministry of hospitality, or teaching Sunday school. Even teaching personal Bible studies can be done from your home. When my children were small, we worked on the Joy bus. I'll always remember the leadership our son, Murray, at age 13, provided on the bus helping out with the younger children and teaching Bible stories. On Saturday, our two oldest daughters, Vonda and Marla, would help pass out the Joy bus news and invite children to ride the bus. They were about ten and eight years old. Misti, our youngest, age two, was too little to be much help, but she loved all the activity. I'll never forget her standing up on the

front seat of the bus facing the children and singing
the books of the Bible to win a prize. What fun! Oh yes,
that was before the days of stressing the wearing of
seat belts. When our children were teens, we worked
with the youth group. On-the-job training is better than
just teaching with words, and we all had lots of fun
doing it.

Michael Gifford in his book *The ABC'S of Family
Life* makes the following statement:

> Evangelism is needed in our homes today. It has been
> said that the church is always just one generation away
> from apostasy. I'm thinking now of a great and faithful
> soldier of Christ who passed from this life some years
> ago. His granddaughter has a lifestyle that brings shame
> to the Lord and would certainly have brought it to this
> marvelous Christian. How did it happen? Who was
> responsible? The answers to those questions are
> unknown to me, but this clearly demonstrates the fact
> that in only a couple generations, a family can go away
> from the truth if care is not taken (35).

You will notice that your ministry may change over
the years. When your children are small, they should
be your number one ministry. In later years, it will be
a different ministry. As I reflect on my own life, I see
how my ministries have changed. First my children
were my priority ministry. Then, for many years my
position as a preacher's wife was my priority ministry,
and now writing and teaching have become my priority
ministry. I incorporate other ministries as time allows,
but I know my priorities.

Enjoy your ministry of raising a Christian family.
Put the family first and do other ministries if you can.
The years go by quickly, and before you know it the
children are grown and you have plenty of time left
for other ministries.

— NOTES —

Discussion Questions

1. Does it take the pressure off, for you and others to recognize your family as your ministry? Does this help you say "no" and not feel guilty?

2. Are there other ministries in which you can involve the whole family? List.

3. What effect do you feel working together in a ministry would have on the family?

4. What do you think about writing down Scriptures and posting them in your house?

5. Why do parents place so much importance on their children being popular?

6. Are you encouraging your children to become preachers, Bible-class teachers and missionaries? Why or why not?

7. Are you taking this ministry seriously? Discuss the seriousness.

8. Discuss how we can let go of the unimportant and take hold of the important things in life.

9. Has your ministry changed as your children grew older? What changes can you see for your future?

10. Discuss the woman in Proverbs 31:10-31

❖ CHAPTER FIVE ❖

Women in Ministries of Hospitality

One of the most important ministries in which a woman can be involved is the showing of hospitality. It can be your greatest ministry for the church. It should be listed along with teaching, personal work, and other women's ministries. It can be a fun form of evangelism. Do you know of a better way to reach out to your friends and neighbors and introduce them to Jesus Christ than to have them in the comfort of your home to relax and laugh together? Many times women do not recognize this as a ministry.

According to *An Expository Dictionary of New Testament Words* by W.E. Vine, hospitality means "love of strangers" (492). The word comes from the Greek word "philos" which means brotherly love. Many areas of church work need open homes to fulfill the work. Teen groups need a warm fireplace by which to sing and pray. Newcomers to church and the community need to be in homes to get better acquainted. Senior members need open homes to help them feel a part of things. Ladies' Bible classes meet in homes to have a less formal atmosphere and therefore share more openly, and friends and neighbors grow closer together by being in each other's homes.

Hospitality in our homes is necessary if the church is to grow as it should. If it is left out, we will develop impersonal relationships. Speaking to people on Sunday morning and asking how they are doing is not the answer. Smith Kite, a preacher and friend, once made the statement, "To really get to know someone you must be in their home, sit in their chairs, eat at their table. You then learn how they think and feel and are more aware of their problems." I can visit a church one time and tell you what kind of relationships the people have who assemble there. If they tarry afterwards and talk and laugh, they are most likely in each others' lives, hearts, and homes. If the lights are out within five minutes of the last amen and the parking lot is empty shortly afterwards, you can bet they do not know one another. It appears these people come to church out of a command and not because they are a true family of God. On the other hand, if the members are around for an hour or so after the closing prayer, talking and loving one another, and then meet at the coffee shop, or restaurant, for another hour, you can be sure they are developing meaningful relationships because they are in each other's lives.

Your ministry of hospitality can be done without leaving the boundaries of your home. This is a perfect ministry for women who have small children. One woman I know, who has several children and can't be involved as much as she would like, has a spare room that she keeps ready for any weary soul who needs a resting place. Preachers, speakers, friends, and family have rested there. She invites weak members of the church over in order to give encouragement, and new members over to get acquainted. She does not conduct seminars, or lead a woman's organization. She attends church and Bible study regularly, but she is not a formal leader. Still, she has a ministry and she works it right out of her home.

One woman moved into a new neighborhood and immediately began to plan a time to have all the neighbors over for a barbecue. She wanted to get acquainted, but more than that she wanted a chance to study the Bible with them. She knew when you care about people they will be more apt to listen. She made invitations and distributed them in her neighborhood. She made a point of talking about spiritual things in her life. Although this scared some away, it helped her find the seekers who needed someone to study the Word with them. The women enjoyed it so much they wanted to make it a weekly event. The result was a neighborhood of women studying the Bible together. This served two basic needs: they learned about God and they developed strong friendships with other women.

Some of the most effective teaching I have been involved in was in an informal setting brought about by a hospitable woman. Through her love and hospitality she made a friend, asked her to come for a study, invited other Christian women to join them to build relationships, and taught her the love of Jesus from the Bible and her own life story.

When the children were little, I always prepared a big Sunday dinner. Many times we invited some of the visitors, or new members, over to our house. You are probably thinking they did not come because they did not know us. Yes, they did! They were overwhelmed by our friendliness. If they were church hunting, it usually helped bring them back. One young, single man visited the assembly and came to dinner. We had met him while car shopping for our daughter. He had not been raised in a close family and had not lived near his family for some time. His words at dinner were, "So this is a family dinner!" We began to study with him. He became a Christian. He began to bring his girlfriend to church and she also became a Christian.

Hospitality is a great way to show love. Because families keep so busy with work and material things, little hospitality is shown today. Your guests will be overwhelmed with your caring attitude. Paul gives us instructions in Romans:

> Love must be sincere. Hate what is evil; cling to what is good. Be devoted to one another in brotherly love. Honor one another above yourselves. Never be lacking in zeal, but keep your spiritual fervor, serving the Lord. Be joyful in hope, patient in affliction, faithful in prayer. Share with God's people who are in need. Practice hospitality (12:9-13).

I remember a family who showed hospitality to my family when I was a small child. My dad was often away from home and mom managed the seven children. One day in late summer, we all decided to walk the mile across the field to a good friend's house. Now, how would you feel if you looked out your front door and saw eight people coming for lunch unexpectedly? Well, if Paul and Pauline Wherry were not glad to see us, they sure fooled us. She prepared a delicious lunch and we had a great day of fun and fellowship that I will never forget.

Many times when my husband is preaching in a Gospel meeting, we stay in the home of one of the members. You really get to know people when you live with them for a week. One such meeting was in Mt. Pleasant, Texas. We stayed in the home of Gene and Billie Campbell. Out of the warmth of their home developed a beautiful friendship we will always cherish. Oh, we met a lot of other nice people, too, but as it has been said, "You have to sit in their chairs and eat at their tables."

True hospitality is not just opening our homes to our friends, sweet as that is. It involves much more. It is opening our homes to strangers, also: "Do not forget to entertain strangers, for by doing so people are entertaining angels without knowing it" (Heb. 13:2). Jesus said, "When you have a luncheon or dinner, do not invite your friends, your brothers or relatives, or your rich neighbors; if you do, they may invite you back and so you will be repaid. But when you give a banquet, invite the poor, the crippled, the lame, the blind, and you will be repaid at the resurrection of the righteous" (Luke 14:12-14). Many times we shun those who have some loathsome disease, or disturbed mind. These people are sometimes outcast. They have no one to love and care for them. Holidays are very difficult because they are lonely. One woman plans a Thanksgiving feast every year on the Sunday before Thanksgiving. She invites all the lonely people she can find. She also chooses a day during the Christmas holidays for the same type of dinner. I wonder whom Jesus would visit if He came to our town? We have an example of Him having compassion for the hungry and providing food for them:

> When Jesus heard what had happened, he withdrew
> by boat privately to a solitary place. Hearing of this,
> the crowds followed him on foot from the towns. When

Jesus landed and saw a large crowd, he had compassion on them and healed their sick.

As evening approached, the disciples came to him and said, 'This is a remote place, and it's already getting late. Send the crowds away, so they can go to the villages and buy themselves some food.'

Jesus replied, 'They do not need to go away. You give them something to eat.'

'We have here only five loaves of bread and two fish,' they answered.

'Bring them here to me,' he said. And he directed the people to sit down on the grass. Taking the five loaves and the two fish and looking up to heaven, he gave thanks and broke the loaves. Then he gave them to the disciples, and the disciples gave them to the people. They all ate and were satisfied, and the disciples picked up twelve basketfuls of broken pieces that were left over (Matt. 14:13-20).

Jesus also entertained and taught people in homes. He made the statement: "...Foxes have holes and birds of the air have nests, but the Son of Man has no place to lay his head" (Matt. 8:20). While he did not have a home of his own, he took advantage of other Christians' homes. In the Bible we find him in the home of Levi (Luke 5:29) and Zacchaeus (Luke 19:5). Much hospitality was shown to Jesus by the brethren. Since they did not have church buildings in New Testament times, the home became the center for teaching, encouraging, and developing maturity in those who came.

Martha is a Bible example of a woman who showed hospitality at a dinner prepared for Jesus and others: "Six days before the Passover, Jesus arrived at Bethany, where Lazarus lived, whom Jesus had raised from the dead. Here a dinner was given in Jesus' honor. Martha served, while Lazarus was among those reclining at the table with him" (John 12:1,2).

I have heard women say, "But my home is private. It's for me and my husband and children. It's the only place we can be alone and I don't want intruders." These women are missing out on some of the most beautiful times in life. Although the home is for the family—a place where they love, laugh, and play together—the family will become closer and will be greatly blessed from sharing. I know this to be true from personal experiences with my own family. My children were raised in an "open" home. We enjoyed many interesting people. I think they would tell you it was a blessing instead of a nuisance.

Others say, "It's too much trouble always having people in. You have to clean and bake all the time, and it is expensive." We need to realize that we don't always have to have things perfect. Let them see us as we really are. Being a perfect housekeeper, being a gourmet cook, and knowing the proper way to fold napkins is nice and can add beauty to your efforts, but these things are not necessary to have a successful hospitality ministry. If you are concerned about the cost of a dinner, then you, as the hostess, plan the meal and ask your guests to bring a dish. Also, there will be times when you serve only coffee and dessert. Most times "less is best." Keep it simple. Sometimes the best friendships develop around the breakfast table rather than a formal dining room table with crystal and china.

I heard one woman say having people in to her home would wear out her new carpet. She was afraid she would not have the money to replace it. I asked her who made it possible for her to have the carpet in the first place. She wanted to tell me she had worked hard for it, but she knew where I was going with the

conversation. She hesitantly said, "God made it possible."
I said, "And don't you think He is powerful enough to
provide it for you again if you wear it out serving
Him?"

We should never let the lack of money keep us from
being hospitable. If we are not hospitable with a little
money, we probably would not be hospitable if we had
much money. One lady told me she had a large crowd
over and suddenly realized she did not have enough
food. The guests were in the living room. She and her
daughter were in the kitchen. They prayed that the
food would be enough. They had food left over. This
happened in the Bible to the widow at Zarephath. God
provides when we step out to do what he asks:

> Some time later the brook dried up because there
> had been no rain in the land. Then the word of the
> Lord came to him: 'Go at once to Zarephath of Sidon
> and stay there. I have commanded a widow in that
> place to supply you with food.' So he went to Zarephath.
> When he came to the town gate, a widow was there
> gathering sticks. He called to her and asked, 'Would you
> bring me a little water in a jar so I may have a drink?'
> As she was going to get it, he called, 'And bring me,
> please, a piece of bread.'
>
> 'As surely as the Lord your God lives,' she replied, 'I
> don't have any bread--only a handful of flour in a jar
> and a little oil in a jug. I am gathering a few sticks to
> take home and make a meal for myself and my son,
> that we may eat it--and die.' Elijah said to her, 'Don't be
> afraid. Go home and do as you have said. But first make
> a small cake of bread for me, and then make something
> for yourself and your son. For this is what the Lord, the
> God of Israel, says; the jar of flour will not be used up
> and the jug of oil will not run dry until the day the

Lord gives rain on the land.' She went away and did as Elijah had told her. So there was food every day for Elijah and for the woman and her family. For the jar of flour was not used up and the jug of oil did not run dry, in keeping with the word of the Lord spoken by Elijah (1 Kings 17:7-16).

Is hospitality your ministry? If so, let your elders know your house is open for whatever needs arise. Let your youth minister know the teens can have some of their fellowships there. Invite the senior members over for fellowship, and have some of your ladies' Bible classes at your home. When you have someone who is less fortunate socially or economically in one of these groups, show them extra kindness. When there are new members in your congregation, have them over to your home to get acquainted. Remember to let your elders know you can be depended on to carry this out. If they have four or five families who have told them they plan to have new members over, the elders will not have to plan a program to accomplish this work. It will be done naturally and effectively through hospitable sisters and their families.

How is the ministry of hospitality an evangelistic ministry? By offering your home to members of the church you are building up, encouraging and helping them to mature. Members will bring friends with them who are not Christians. You will have the opportunity to help set up Bible studies with these people. The same is true with visitors to your assembly. When they come to your home, you will find it easy to get into a Bible study. All these things broaden the borders of the kingdom.

Vonette Bright and Barbara Ball, in their book *The Joy of Hospitality*, have this to say: "Whether you are single or married, male or female, live in a house or an apartment, your home is a God-given resource that can be used to touch people in an intimate, personal way. It doesn't matter to God whether your home is elaborate or simple. All He needs is your willingness to love others as He does" (34).

Peter gives us this admonition: "Above all, love each other deeply, because love covers over a multitude of sins. Offer hospitality to one another without grumbling. Each one should use whatever spiritual gift he has received to serve others, faithfully administering God's grace in its various forms" (1 Peter 4:8-10).

So, open your home and your heart to those around you, and use what the Lord has blessed you with as your greatest ministry for the church and to help broaden the borders of the kingdom. You can't take your material things with you, so use them up in the Lord's work. Your life will be richly blessed, both in this life and in the one to come.

Discussion Questions

1. How do you feel about the sharing of your home? Is this a ministry in which you can be comfortable?

2. What strengths and talents has God given you to make hospitality your ministry?

3. What would be the advantages of this ministry?

4. What would be the disadvantages of this ministry?

5. Discuss: Is it necessary to be in each other's homes to be in each other's hearts?

6. Give examples of hospitable women in your congregation and note the effectiveness of their work in the church.

7. Discuss the plight of the widow at Zarephath. Apply this Scripture to your hospitable events.

8. Discuss hospitality shown to the outcast.

9. Discuss hospitable women in the Bible.

10. Is this one of your ministries? Why? Why not?

— NOTES —

❖ CHAPTER SIX ❖

Women in Teaching Ministries

Mary Magdalene and several other women were called by the Lord to take His message to the disciples. The women were headed to the tomb of Jesus. When they got there, they found grave clothes but no body. Jesus had risen. Then, when they recognized Jesus in the garden, He sent them on a very important mission. He told them to go and tell the other brethren to go to Galilee and they would see Him. Jesus could have revealed himself to anyone, for the first time after his resurrection, to take this important message, but he chose women. Does this tell us something about what He expects of us? The account reads:

> After the Sabbath, at dawn on the first day of the week, Mary Magdalene and the other Mary went to look at the tomb.
>
> There was a violent earthquake, for an angel of the Lord came down from heaven and, going to the tomb, rolled back the stone and sat on it. His appearance was like lightning, and his clothes were white as snow. The

guards were so afraid of him that they shook and became like dead men.

The angel said to the women, 'Do not be afraid, for I know that you are looking for Jesus, who was crucified. He is not here; he has risen, just as he said. Come and see the place where he lay. Then go quickly and tell his disciples: 'He has risen from the dead and is going ahead of you into Galilee. There you will see him.' Now I have told you.

So the women hurried away from the tomb, afraid yet filled with joy, and ran to tell his disciples. Suddenly Jesus met them. 'Greetings,' he said. They came to him, clasped his feet and worshipped him. Then Jesus said to them, 'Do not be afraid. Go and tell my brothers to go to Galilee; there they will see me' (Matt. 28:1-10).

As Christian women, our first concern after we have seen the Lord through studying His word should be to go and tell someone else just as Mary did. This ministry is not just for the extroverted woman. "For out of the overflow of the heart the mouth speaks" (Matt. 12:34b). The mouth will speak if we fall in love with Jesus because then, and only then, will we have an overflow. Women talk about what they love. Our overflow leads us to talk about our children, our grandchildren, and our favorite hobby. Why then would our love for the Lord not lead us to talk about Him? To whom do we talk? Anyone with whom we come in contact: the clerk at the grocery store, the beautician at the beauty shop, and the postman. You never know who the Lord is sending to you unless you speak. We should make an effort to be alert to people. I have gone through a grocery store line all wrapped up in myself and my day's activities and never looked at the clerk. Somehow I managed to put all my groceries on the conveyor belt, wrote my check, gave it to her, and took my groceries out of the store, and never looked into her face. This is sad. I need to talk with her about how her day is going, and if I go through her check-out line enough times, I will get the opportunity to talk to her about the Lord.

"We are therefore Christ's ambassadors, as though God were making his appeal through us..." (2 Cor. 5:20). What is an ambassador? An ambassador for the United States represents this country, provides our viewpoint, and is our voice to other countries. As Christ's ambassador, we represent Him to others. We are His voice. Are we good ambassadors for the Lord? Is He satisfied with the way we represent Him?

Women are not exempt from the Great Commission. Jesus said, "...go and make disciples of all nations, baptizing them in the name of the Father and of the Son and of the Holy Spirit, and teaching them to obey everything I have commanded you..." (Matt. 28:19,20). The "them" is "us," including women. In the church where I attend, the women take this command of the Lord very seriously. A large percentage of us teach personal Bible studies one-on-one to women with whom we come in contact. We receive contacts from church visitors, acquaintances of new converts, and new people we meet daily. How do we get the study? We ask! We say, "We are having a Bible study. Would you like to come?" After a woman has visited the assembly, we say, "We're so glad you visited with us today. Can we get together to answer any questions that may have arisen from your being here?" Remember, we must develop an overflow. Then it will be much easier to speak up and ask for the study.

After you have been successful in setting up a study with a new woman, never go on the study alone. Take with you a woman who is already a Christian, but who needs training to lead the studies. She will receive the necessary training and she will also develop a relationship with the new woman. When the new woman attends church, she will already know you and the trainee. This will take away the stress from coming to a new place because she already has friends there. It is a good idea to have a luncheon or tea to introduce her to other women.

As soon as a new woman has finished the studies and becomes a Christian, and has learned about the mission of the church and our personal mission on Earth, we have her thinking of who she plans to share the Gospel with. Everyone knows someone who is searching. Have her make a list. Start praying about the list with her. Encourage her to start telling the people on her list about the changes that have occurred in her life and about the church she has found. Have her involved in the studies with her friends. She will be learning to teach also.

You may be thinking, "In our church, the preacher does the teaching." I often ask this question when I am teaching in a women's workshop: "If a woman walked into your assembly alone and asked what she needed to do to be a member of the church, who would teach her?" The answer is usually, "Our preacher." Now, why would you send the preacher to teach a woman? It's no wonder so many preachers get into trouble. The older women are to teach and train the younger women: "...teach the older women to be reverent in the way they live, not to be slanderers or addicted to much wine, but to teach what is good. Then they can train the younger women to love their husbands and children, to be self-controlled and pure, to be busy at home, to be kind, and to be subject to their husbands, so that no one will malign the word of God" (Titus 2:3-5). In our congregation, if a couple comes, a couple teaches. If a man comes, a man teaches, and if a woman comes, a woman teaches. Woman will usually be more personal and share their hearts better with another woman. Great relationships can be developed.

Sometimes women feel they have to know everything before they can teach. Not so. We have a study series. I call it a cheat sheet. I don't have to remember every Scripture and every detail that I want to discuss. I have it on a paper before me as we open the Bible and study the Word together. (Because of the request of many women, I have enclosed some of these lessons at the end of this chapter). I like to create a very informal and comfortable atmosphere around my kitchen table. If the woman is not a believer, we start with a study about Christian evidences. We study about Jesus and what He has done for us, and the fact that He has all authority. If she is a strong believer, we go to the Gospel study more quickly. But first, we always go over the sin lists in the Bible. In today's world, people are confused as to what is right and wrong. We must establish that the Bible is the complete authority and read it to find out how God expects us to live. You will be surprised to find out that people do not know.

If you are a woman who has never led someone to the Lord, you are missing out on one of the greatest blessings of being a Christian. In fact, the Bible says by being active in sharing our faith we will have a full understanding of every good thing: "I pray that you may be active in sharing your faith, so that you will have a full understanding of every good thing we have in Christ" (Philemon 1:6). I want a full understanding of every good thing, don't you? Remember, it's not an option for the Christian. It's a command. Is it obvious that this is the ministry I'm the most excited about?

Setting Up Studies with Visitors

When a church is growing and reaching out to the community, visitors come to see what is going on. If it is unified and serious about taking the Gospel to the world, God will send the visitors. They may be looking for a church, and through the influence of the members and advertisement, they keep hearing about you. They come to visit. What happens then? Whether they return depends on you. If the visitor is a woman, the women of the church should know that they are the ones to follow up with her. We need to let her know that she is welcome and we are concerned for her. Here are a few guidelines for following up with a visitor:

1. In your "Women in Teaching Ministries" group you may have a leader who collects the names of women who visit and gives them out to the group for follow-up. If your church is small, you should meet each visitor so you will know the person you are assigned. This may not be possible in larger congregations. If you do not have a ministry group, you are on your own.

2. Always be alert at church for visitors, especially the women. Greet them and get acquainted. Help them find classrooms for their children. Show them around.

3. If there is no leader to give you a name, ask the record-keeper or the secretary for the phone number of the women visitors.

4. A few days after she visited, call her on the phone. Tell her that you are from the _____ church. Ask if she has a few minutes to talk with you. If you have caught her at a bad time, call back later.

5. Tell her that you appreciate her visit. Let her know that you are glad she came on Sunday. Ask how she happened to visit the church.

6. Ask if she needs information about anything: classes, programs, Bible studies. Does she have questions about the class she attended or the teacher? Maybe she wants to know the teacher's name. Give her all the information she wants.

7. If you have a women's program, tell her about it and ask her to be a part. Ask her to attend your next group meeting to see how it works. She may not have interest in the same ministry as you do, but it will help her see what the women's ministry is all about.

8. Ask if she would like to join a small group Bible study. If she says yes and you are not yet leading studies, set up the study and call your group leader. She will know who is available to lead a study. If you do not have a women's program, call someone you know is prepared to lead the studies. Go along on the studies for training and relationship building.

9. If you are leading the study, always take someone with you for training and to develop relationships.

10. Make sure your elders are aware of your "Women in Teaching Ministries" program so they will know this work is being done. If you are not in a program,

but have made this one of your priority ministries, let your elders know.

11. Be faithful, consistent, and dependable in following through with the studies.

12. Rejoice with her, other members of the church, and the angels in heaven when she becomes a Christian.

Teaching Children

Teaching Bible class is an important and rewarding ministry for women in the church. Do you love children? Could this be the ministry to which God is calling you? There are many things of importance in being a teacher, all of which you have read in your teacher's manuals or heard about at teachers' workshops. The teacher must be a living visual aid. Her life speaks louder than her words. Her students need to see Jesus in everything she does and says. They need to see Christian living in action. Her natural conversation must show that she prays and reads her Bible and that she has a sincere love for the lost.

The curriculum is also very important. The lessons should be chosen based on the ages and needs of the students. The brotherhood has provided us with beautifully designed lessons for all ages to make our job easier. If time permits, homemade visuals are always great.

Just as important as the teacher being a Christian and having good lesson material, is her attitude. Some people say a good attitude is the most important of all. You might say: "But if she is a Christian she will have a good attitude." Really? Smiles and greetings by name when the students arrive in class are necessities. The teacher who isn't there to smile and greet when her students arrive should be removed.

Go the extra mile for your students. Remember their birthdays in a special way. If they are not in class, find out why. Tape your class, the story, and comments of the students, and take or send it to anyone who was absent because of illness.

Be alert to the needs of your students, and be willing to talk with parents when needs arise. Know your students' parents. When new students attend, meet the parents. It will help the entire family feel welcome if they meet the children's teachers right in the beginning.

If you are successfully showing Christ in your life, teaching and having the right attitude, you may feel you are doing a great job, and you are, but your ministry could expand. Think about broadening your ministry even more.

Usually there are a few children in your classroom whose parents do not attend church. It may be that they come with friends or ride a bus. This is an open door for you. Many teachers never meet the parents of these children. Make efforts to get acquainted. A letter, phone call, or visit can be beneficial. Usually, this is a door open wide because you are the child's teacher. Parents are receptive to a teacher of their children. You have something to talk about of mutual interest, their child. You can also share with them the material you will be teaching their child. This opens the door wider for establishing grounds for possibly a future Bible study with the parents. Invite them to an open house or a parent-child outing. Many parents are in church today because of a Bible teacher. In our church, we have several members whose children attended first and later, through outreach, the parents came.

If your ministry is teaching children, you can also be an effective Bible teacher to children in your neighborhood. Many times we don't want to be bothered with the child next door. We hear all kinds of excuses. I can tell you a true story that will help you realize the importance of one little neighborhood girl.

I was eight years old when my family moved next door to Mable Mann. I soon found out that Mable went to church every Sunday and I asked her if I could go along. She was delighted to have me go. She didn't use excuses as to why she couldn't take me, although she had plenty. Little did I realize that behind her pretty smile was concern for how either of us would get there if she started taking me. But Mable was a woman with a mission. She knew the importance of saving a soul. She believed the Scripture when it says, "But seek first his kingdom and his righteousness, and all these things will be given to you as well" (Matt. 6:33).

The first Sunday she picked me up in the new car she usually drove to church. She seemed a little concerned when we saw her husband as we drove through town. The next Sunday she picked me up in the pickup truck her husband usually drove. When we drove through town, her husband was sitting in the new car on Main Street, reading the newspaper. The third Sunday, her husband took the keys to the pickup and left in the car. As we left the farm in one of the farm trucks used to haul grain, I noticed a tractor by the barn and I wondered if we would be going to church on it next week. The next week passed, Sunday morning came, and Mable called one of the deacons of the church to come to pick us up. Years later I found out the problem. Her husband didn't want her going to church and he certainly didn't want her taking the neighbor kids along.

Now, what would you have done? It would have been so easy to just say, "I'm sorry, but I can't take you. My husband won't let me." We give up so easily when there is conflict or when it is inconvenient for us. Inconvenient? Christ was certainly inconvenienced for us, wasn't he?

I spent many hours at Mable's house. She helped me get my Sunday school lessons and answered all my questions. Soon my older brother started going to church. Today he is a preacher. Not long after that my mother started going and my younger brothers and sister. All of us became Christians through the determination of one evangelistic woman. Have I returned the favor? How could I live with myself if the answer was no? Our cars have been transportation for many children. Sometimes we drove both cars in order to take more children. There are several adult members of our church who came with us as children. Just this past year a young man died while mountain climbing in Alaska. He was a neighborhood boy who started going to church with us when he was about four years old. He grew up in the church, attending without his family.

Women, if you have chosen teaching children as your ministry in the church, please feel good about it, do the best job possible, know how important your work is, and do it all to the glory of God. When someone asks you what you do as a woman out there at that church, don't say, "Oh, the men do most of the work. Women aren't allowed to do much." Say, "I'm an evangelistic woman. I'm a Bible class teacher. I have a very important position in that church. Come with me and I'll show you what I do."

Molding Live

I took a piece of plastic clay,
And idly fashioned it one day;
And as my fingers pressed it still,
It moved and yielded to my will.
I came again when days were past,
The bit of clay was hard at last;
The form I gave it still it bore,
But I could change that form no more.

I took a piece of living clay,
And gently formed it day by day;
And molded with my power and art,
A young child's soft and yielding heart.
I came again when years were gone,
It was a man I looked upon;
He still that early impress wore,
But I could change him nevermore.
                                    —Anonymous

Discussion Questions

1. How do you feel about being Christ's ambassador?

2. Do you feel women sometimes relate better to women in studying the Bible, than men relate to women? Why? Why not?

3. Are you an extroverted person? If so, you are being called to be a dynamic personal worker. If not, you are still being called. The Holy Spirit has changed many timid hearts to bold ones for the Lord. How do you feel about this?

4. What are your greatest strengths for teaching other women about the Lord?

5. What is holding you back from this ministry?

6. Would you be willing to help organize a teaching ministry?

7. Do you take pride in your role as a teacher of children? Do you realize what an important job you are doing? Explain.

8. What are your greatest strengths for a children's ministry?

9. Why do you think some women prefer to teach adults?

10. Can you broaden your ministry by reaching out to a child who isn't learning about God in any other way?

I do not know where these study sheets originated. We have used them for many years and changes have been made periodically in the format.

Study Sheet #1

Spiritual Lifeline

Purpose:

To help an individual identify significant spiritual events that have occurred in her life. To use later in determining any discrepancies between the biblical pattern of a relationship with God and her own.

Note: The spiritual lifeline should be the first discussion in your study because many people do not know what they believe. When you tell them what the Bible teaches, they may say that is what they believe they have done. The lifeline helps you as the teacher know where they are and aids you in taking them where they need to go, to the cross of Christ.

Introduction:

Explain that before you start studying the Bible, you would like for her to share some information about herself. Ask, "Have you ever made a lifeline about yourself? You know, when you were born, married, etc.?" Then add, "Today, I want to make a spiritual lifeline about you. It will include some of those same things, but also more details about things like what church you may have attended when you were a child." Draw a line on the paper. It sometimes helps to share some of your own spiritual lifeline if a person is reluctant to share.

1. Where were you born?

2. Were you baptized as an infant? If so, in what church?

3. What was your parents' religious affiliation? Do you share those beliefs today?

4. Did you attend church as a child? Where?

5. What has been your spiritual involvement since then? Have you attended church regularly at any time during your life?

6. What were other spiritual turning points or special experiences in your life?

7. When in your life, if ever, have you felt lost? Why? Do you consider yourself saved? (Three possible answers: yes, no, and don't know.)

8. If I were to place a cross at the point you were saved on this line, where would I put it? Tell me the story. What happened? Were your sins forgiven? Were you baptized? Why? How? Did you make Jesus your Lord? Where do you stand with God right now?

Conclusion:

Thank her for sharing. Tell her you are looking forward to studying with her. Assure her that the Bible says we can know we are saved and that we have eternal life (1 John 5:13). Tell her you are going to put the paper away and refer to it later in the studies.

Study Sheet #2

Seeking God

Purpose:

To learn the importance of seeking God. To learn to seek Him on His terms, not our own. To see Bible examples of seekers.

Introduction:

1. Read Matthew 7:7. What are we promised? Why is this one of the greatest promises in the world? What things are seekers looking for today? (Money, marriage, love, happiness, fun, fame, inner peace, to make their own rules concerning their salvation.)

2. Read Matthew 7:13,14. If seekers are promised they will find eternal life, and only a few find it, how many people are truly seeking God? (Few.)

3. Read Hebrews 11:6. What does God expect us to do about seeking him? (To be earnest and diligent.)

4. Read Matthew 6:33. What are we to seek first? What kinds of things keep us from seeking God first and making this the top priority? (Friends, family, job, school, etc.)

Biblical Examples of People Seeking God:

1. The Ethiopian — Acts 8:26-40. He is an important man who is very busy, but he still made time for God. He was seeking in the right place, the Scriptures. He kept studying even though he was not sure of what he was reading. He was humble because he

asks for help. When he finds the answers, he stops seeking and acts. He is happy after he has come to know God.

2. The Bereans — Acts 17:11. They searched the Scriptures daily.

3. The Man in the Field — Matthew 13:44. He was not actively seeking but stumbled on the truth. He was happy about finding it. He sold everything. (Commitment.)

4. The Merchant — Matthew 13:45. He was looking for the fine pearls (actively seeking). He sold everything (commitment) to obtain the pearls.

Conclusion:

What do we learn from these Scriptures about seeking God? What did the people do when they found the truth? Let's be active seekers. Let's look in the right places.

Study Sheet #3

A Study of Sin

Purpose:

In today's world the definition of sin has been blurred. That is why we must go to the Bible to see what is right and wrong. This lesson is to help people understand what sin is, identify their sinful condition, and instill in them a desire to rid their lives of sin.

Introduction:

As we go through the sin list, feel free to share about your life. I will be sharing with you the things in which God has helped me overcome and the things in which I continue to struggle. Remember, all of us are sinners (Rom. 3:23). Only Jesus was sinless (Heb. 4:15). But now as Christians, we are to hate sin, stop practicing sin, and with the help of the Holy Spirit, do our best to get it out of our lives (Col. 3:5). The wages of sin is death (Rom. 6:23). Jesus can rescue us from this death (Rom. 7:24,25).

Sin List in the Bible:

Mark 7:20; Galatians 5:19-21; Romans 1:18-32; 1 Corinthians 6:9-10; Ephesians 4:31, 5:3; Col. 3:5-10

Evil Thoughts: Morally bad or wrong.

Sexual Immorality: Any sex outside marriage.

Theft: Taking what is not yours. Stealing.

Murder: To kill.

Adultery: Sex between people who are not married to each other.

Greed: Excessive desire for getting or having wealth without thought of others.

Malice: Active ill will or hatred towards another.

Deceit: To represent what is not true.

Lewdness: Intending to excite in sexual desires.

Envy: Hatred, jealousy, ill will.

Slander: To damage a person's reputation by telling others a false statement.

Arrogance: Overbearing pride or self-importance.

Folly: A foolish action or belief.

Impurity: To defile or contaminate; unchaste, impure thoughts.

Debauchery: Extreme indulgence in one's appetites, especially sensual pleasure.

Idolatry: Anything that stands between you and God.

Witchcraft: The practice of witches, black magic, astrology, horoscopes, etc.

Hatred: To harbor ill will or to despise, loathe, or detest someone.

Discord: To cause trouble, quarrel; lack of harmony.

Jealousy: To resent someone or her influence.

Rage: A furious, uncontrolled anger.

Selfish Ambition: Consumed by worldly aspirations.

Dissension: Bitter rifts between parties.

Factions: A clique within the main body causing divisions in the group.

Drunkenness: Intoxication, loss of control by means of alcohol, drugs, etc.

Study Sheet #4

The Cross Study

Purpose:

To show how much God loves us. To gain a deep appreciation for the physical, emotional, and spiritual pain Jesus endured in order for us to be reconciled to God.

Introduction:

God loved us so much that He gave His son for us (John 3:16). Would we give our son to save anyone? Jesus went through much suffering to be our perfect sacrifice for sin.

Read Matthew 26:36-27:54.

Jesus Suffered Emotional Pain:

Jesus was overwhelmed with sorrow and troubled. He fell with his face to the ground to pray. He asked the Father if it was possible to take the crucifixion away. He was alone. His friends could not stay awake to hold his hand in this crucial hour. Think of a time when you were the most overwhelmed with sorrow. Can you sympathize with Jesus?

Jesus Suffered Physical Pain:

What is the most physical pain you have ever endured? Were you in a car accident or injured? Jesus went through much physical pain for us. He was stripped of his clothes and beaten. A crown of thorns was placed on his head. He was struck on the head again and again. He was crucified on a cross.

Jesus Suffered Spiritual Pain:

Jesus died for all our sins. He became sin for us. God could not look upon sin. He had to leave his Son alone to die. Jesus said, "My God, why have you forsaken me?" Have you ever felt separated from God because of your sins?

Conclusion:

After Jesus finished His work on earth, He went back to the Father awaiting the day when Christians will be with Him in heaven (Hebrews 1:1-4). He has done all He can for us. It is up to us to accept Him. How do you feel about all He went through for us?

Study Sheet #5

What Must I Do to Be Saved?

Purpose:

If you asked several people what to do to be saved, you would get different answers. We want to know what the Bible says.

Introduction:

The Bible says we can know that we have eternal life (1 John 5:13).

We Must Have Faith:

Faith is believing God even when you don't understand or see Him.

- We can't please God without faith (Heb. 11:6).
- How does one obtain faith? (Rom. 10:14-17)
- What do you need to believe? (John 8:24)

We Must Repent:

Repentance means a change of mind that produces a change of direction.

- What does the Bible say about repentance? (Acts 2:37,38)
- What does it mean to repent? (Luke 13:3; Acts 3:19)
- What do you need to make up your mind to do? (Col. 3:5-11)
- What does true repentance come from? (2 Cor. 7:8-11)

We Must Confess:

Confession means to tell others about Jesus being your Lord.

- What do we need to do? (Rom. 10:9,10)
- What do we need to confess? (Matt. 10:32,33)

We Must Be Baptized:

To be baptized means to obey the death, burial, and resurrection of Christ. Baptism is a burial. It comes from the Greek word "baptizo" which means to immerse, dip, or plunge.

- You must obey the Gospel (2 Thess. 1:7-9).
- What is the Gospel? (1 Cor. 15:1-4)
- How do I obey it? (Rom. 6:3,4) I become clothed with Christ (Gal. 3:26,27).

Conclusion:

When we obey the Gospel (are baptized) we are reenacting Jesus' death, burial, and resurrection. At this point in time three great blessings are given to us: remission of sins, the indwelling Holy Spirit, and admission to the Lord's church (Acts 2:38,47). What more could we ask? Have you obeyed the Gospel?

Study Sheet #6

Counting the Costs

Purpose:

To help each one understand the cost of becoming a Christian. It is not to be taken lightly. A person should not go through the motions if she is not serious. She must plan to do everything in her power to live for the Lord and to get sinful things out of her life.

Introduction:

Before getting involved in anything, we want to know what it costs. Salvation does not cost anything, but it cost everything. Our salvation cost Jesus a terrible death. To be a Christian means to be a disciple. A disciple is someone who wants to be just like Jesus. It is an every day, every minute thing. It is not easy. But it is worth it.

We Must Do Whatever He Says:

Simon had fished all night and had caught no fish. Jesus told him to put down his nets again. Simon reminded Jesus that they had worked hard all night and had not caught anything. But he told Jesus "because you say so, I will let down the nets again." When they did this, they caught many fish. Many times we do not know why Jesus says for us to do certain things. But a true disciple obeys even if she does not understand. Jesus blesses us for it just as he did Simon. Simon did not understand, and he probably did not think they would catch fish, but he wanted to obey Jesus anyway (Luke 5:1-11). This is the attitude we must have.

What Would Stand in Your Way of Becoming a Disciple?:

- Relationships — Do you have worldly friends or family with whom you could not participate in sinful things any more?
- Would your job stand in your way? Do you have time to be a Christian?
- Do you have sinful habits you are not willing to give up (Col. 3:5)?
- Are you willing to study the Bible and pray often (Acts 17:11; 1 Thess. 5:17)?
- Are you willing to tell your friends about finding the Lord (2 Cor. 5:20)?
- Will you be committed to the body and the church, and place yourself under its elders (Heb. 10:25; Heb. 13:7,17)?
- Are you willing to support the works of the church monetarily (Luke 6:38, 1 Tim. 6:10)?

Conclusion:

If the person you are studying with is ready to commit her life to Christ and be baptized, have as many brothers and sisters there as possible to celebrate the new birth, no matter what time it is.

Study Sheet #7

A Study of the Church

Purpose:

To show what the Bible says about the church. Only churches that follow the plan in the Bible are the true church.

Introduction:

Jesus came to build His church (Matt. 16:15-19). Jesus pleaded before He died that we all be one (John 17:20-23), yet we are very divided. The only way to be one is to follow the plan in the Bible.

- Founder: Christ — Matthew 15:18
- Where: Jerusalem — Isaiah 2:3; Acts 2
- When: A.D. 33
- Head: Christ — Ephesians 1:22
- Made up of:
  Elders — Titus 1:5; 1 Peter 5:1-3; 1
  Timothy 3:1-7;
  Deacons — Acts 6:1-6; 1 Timothy 3:8-13;
  Members — Acts 2:41-47; Colossians 1:13;
  1 Corinthians 1:2.
- Name:
  Church of Christ — Matthew 16:18;
  Church of God — 1 Corinthians 1:2;
  Body of Christ — Colossians 1:18;
  Ephesians 1:23;
  Bride of Christ — Romans 7:4;
  Revelations 21:9.

- Name of its Members:
    Disciples — John 15:8; Acts 11:26;
    Saints — Romans 1:7; 1 Corinthians 1:2;
        Philippians 1:1;
    Brethren — Luke 8:21; Galatians 6:1;
    Children — Galatians 3:26; 1 John 2:1;
    Christians — Acts 11:26; 26:28; 1 Peter 4:16.
- Worship:
    Sing — Colossians 3:16;
    Pray — 1 Thessalonians 5:17;
    Teach — Acts 20:7;
    Commune — 1 Corinthians 11:23;
    Contribute — 1 Corinthians 16:1,2.
- Mission: To glorify God — All these things
    glorify God. Saving souls glorifies God.
    Ephesians 3:10; John 6:45; 1 Timothy 4:16.
- Admission Into: Acts 2
    Paul preached the first recorded gospel
        sermon. V. 14-39
    People heard about the cross and
        resurrection. V. 36
    They were cut to the heart. V. 37
    They repented and made Jesus Lord of
        their life. V. 38,39
    They were baptized. V. 38-41
    They received forgiveness of sins and the
        indwelling Holy Spirit. V. 38
    The Lord added them to His church. V.
        41-47

CHAPTER SEVEN

Women in Benevolent Ministries

Tabitha is one of the first Biblical figures to come to mind when I look for a benevolent woman. She was always doing good and helping the poor. She made robes and other clothing for those in need. She must have been a great help and comfort to the widows, because when she died they all stood around her crying. From the text, I think we can determine that this was her ministry:

> In Joppa there was a disciple named Tabitha (which, when translated, is Dorcas), who was always doing good and helping the poor. About that time she became sick and died, and her body was washed and placed in an upstairs room. Lydda was near Joppa; so when the disciples heard that Peter was in Lydda, they sent two men to him and urged him, "Please come at once!"
>
> Peter went with them, and when he arrived he was taken upstairs to the room. All the widows stood around him, crying and showing him the robes and other

clothing that Dorcas had made while she was still with them.

Peter sent them all out of the room; then he got down on his knees and prayed. Turning toward the dead woman he said, "Tabitha, get up." She opened her eyes, and seeing Peter, she sat up. He took her by the hand and helped her to her feet. Then he called the believers and the widows and presented her to them alive. This became known all over Joppa, and many people believed in the Lord (Acts 9:36-42).

The "worthy woman," as we call her, is another great example. "She opens her arms to the poor and extends her hands to the needy" (Prov. 31:20). The needy and poor will always be with us, and this is a good place for women to serve in the church. Women truly have that special touch to deal with those in need. It must have something to do with our mothering nature.

The word benevolent means "doing good; kind, charitable; a charitable act or gift" (Webster's New World Dictionary of the American Language, College Edition.). The word charity means love. Therefore, a benevolent act is simply an act of love for one in need.

All Christians will be involved in these acts of kindness at some time or another. They come so easily to some people. A few years ago, one of the ladies in our church needed a blue purse to go with a dress that she wanted to wear to her mother's funeral. She wasn't really in a state of mind to go shopping. Later she found three blue purses on her car seat. One young woman whose husband was out of work was taking her children through the drive-thru at a fast food restaurant as a special treat, knowing she shouldn't spend the money. The lady in the car in front of her was a woman from her church. This woman knew that the woman with the children had little money and that she was sacrificing to treat the children. She paid for their food. What a nice surprise when the young lady at the window said, "Yours is already paid."

A woman was lying in her hospital bed. Her husband was at work. He had already taken off the time allowed. Her mother was at home with their three children. She looked out the window at the busy street where cars were speeding by and people were quickly walking to their next appointments. Everything was going on as usual, except her. Her life had come to a standstill. Any minute now the doctor would come in to give her the results of her test. The minutes dragged on to what seemed like hours. There was a knock at the door. The door opened and in walked two women from her church. After hugs were exchanged, one of the women handed her a rose and told her it was for love. The other one led a prayer. They told her that another woman had gone to her mother's house to take care of the children so her mother could take a break. Others were preparing food to take to her house. Oh, beautiful sisters of mercy; what would we do without them?

Caring for the sick is a ministry in which some women have special talents. We are most vulnerable when we are sick. It's a time when we can become lonely. We need someone to understand, someone to listen. We sometimes think the sophisticated and poised woman is exempt from these needs. At times such as these, they don't feel sophisticated or poised. Sometimes these women are the ones who are the most in need. I've known women who make visiting the hospital their ministry. They go sit with the sick, sometimes talking, sometimes listening, sometimes reading to them, and sometimes just sitting quietly.

Remember the story of the Samaritan who took care of the man who had been robbed and beaten? He took pity on him. Pity means sorrow felt for another person's suffering or misfortune, compassion, sympathy, a cause for sorrow or regret. The Samaritan man bandaged his wounds, took him to an inn, and cared for him. We are told to do as he did. Jesus said:

> A man was going down from Jerusalem to Jericho, when he fell into the hands of robbers. They stripped him of clothes, beat him and went away, leaving him half dead. A priest happened to be going down the same road, and when he saw the man, he passed by on the other side. So too, a Levite, when he came to the place and saw him, passed by on the other side. But a Samaritan, as he traveled, came where the man was; and when he saw him, he took pity on him. He went to him and bandaged his wounds, pouring on oil and wine. Then he put the man on his own donkey, took him to an inn and took care of him. The next day he took out two silver coins and gave them to the inn keeper. "Look after him," he said, "and when I return, I will reimburse you for any extra expense you may have" (Luke 10:30-37).

Personally, I have been on both ends when it comes to benevolence, and I must say it is much easier to give than to receive. Twenty-two years ago my husband and I decided to attend a school of preaching in order for him to become a preacher. It took several years to come to this decision. To sell out our farming operation and leave the only place we had ever called home wasn't an easy decision. Many times when a man who already has a family decides to become a preacher, he is supported by other Christians and other churches. The church is great about providing financial support to train preachers. This wasn't too hard to accept because it came weekly or monthly just as a salary. What was hard to accept was when someone took care of those extra things. We were expecting our fourth child while at school. Bad planning, we thought, or no planning. We really didn't know how we were going to pay the doctor and hospital bills, but we had faith that God would provide. And God did provide. A very generous man by the name of Morris Bowman of Newport, Arkansas wrote a check to pay the total charges at the doctor and the hospital. Wow! We were touched at how God used Morris on our behalf. So touched that we named our little girl Misti Morris. We figured lots of girls have their maiden name as their middle name and Morris sounded like that. Besides I always liked to be different where names were concerned. Misti, however, went through a few years of not being too thrilled about her name. Then one day we took her to renew her acquaintance with her namesake. When she saw what a neat Christian man he is, she became very proud of her name. I'm sure Morris and his lovely wife, Violet, have done more of these benevolent acts than we can imagine. They are involved in several ministries, one of them being financial support to train ministers.

"Gifts to the poor have come up as a remembrance before God" (Acts 10:4). Paul says these gifts given in love will be credited to the account of the giver. "For even when I was in Thessalonica, you sent me aid again and again when I was in need. Not that I am looking for a gift, but I am looking for what may be credited to your account" (Phil. 4:16,17). Women helped support Jesus and His apostles monetarily:

> After this, Jesus traveled about from one town and village to another, proclaiming the good news of the kingdom of God. The Twelve were with Him, and also some women who had been cured of evil spirits and

> diseases: Mary, called Magdalene, from whom seven
> demons had come out; Joanna the wife of Cuza, the
> manager of Herod's household; Susanna; and many
> others. These women were helping to support them out
> of their own means (Luke 8:1-3).

In every church, there are needs. As a church grows in number, the needs increase. When a church has only 50 people, everyone chips in and takes care of needs that come up. When a church grows in number, we must be more aware and prepared. Financial crises can come from many different sources. Those who need assistance often include: the sick, those whose houses have burned, those who have lost their jobs, unwed mothers who have been kicked out of their parents' houses, travelers in distress, and men who need financial help to train for the ministry. Sometimes we hear of a family in our church that is struggling financially, and we get the message out for everyone to bring a bag of groceries to Sunday night assembly. We call it a sack shower. We all get into our pantries, fill a bag, and bring it to the foyer of the church building. We usually do not know who is the recipient because sometimes they are embarrassed and the person planning the sack shower does not tell everyone. It is wonderful to see the foyer full of sacks of groceries. James gives us these words to encourage us to help with needs: "Suppose a brother or sister is without clothes and daily food. If one of you says to him, 'Go, I wish you well; keep warm and well fed,' but does nothing about his physical needs, what good is it" (James 2:15,16)?

Women can help in this ministry by working in the church's food pantry or clothing room. If we are going to be prepared when there is a crisis in the church or community, it is necessary for us to be well equipped and supplied. It takes time to gather, sort, and label food and clothing. Some clothing, although useful, is donated needing repairs or laundering. This sounds like hard work. It is. But it's a ministry to the Lord that can benefit many people. Let's look at Jesus' words:

> ..'Depart from me, you who are cursed, into the eternal fire prepared for the devil and his angels. For I was hungry and you gave me nothing to eat, I was thirsty and you gave me nothing to drink, I was a stranger and you did not invite me in, I needed clothes and you did not clothe me, I was sick and in prison and you did not look after me.'
>
> They also will answer, 'Lord, when did we see you hungry or thirsty or a stranger or needing clothes or sick or in prison, and did not help you?'
>
> He will reply, 'I tell you the truth, whatever you did not do for one of the least of these, you did not do for me' (Matt. 25:41-45).

How can this be considered evangelistic? You are reaching out in love and caring, and sometimes through the person in need—or one of their relatives—you will find an opportunity to reach out with the Gospel, especially as your church reaches beyond its walls and into the community.

I know of a church in Wynne, Arkansas, that erected a large metal building on the church's property exclusively for the purpose of benevolence. They are always on the lookout for good used furniture, appliances, clothing, and toys. When someone in town has a burnout, whether members of the church or not, members of the church are the first ones there. The women of the church are a great help in this benevolent ministry.

Nursing home visitation is a work that fits in with benevolent acts of love. There are many lonely people in nursing homes. Sometimes their families are too busy with their own lives to give them the attention they need. Items can be made that they need. Little gifts can be taken. Love can be shared. I know women who go there to sing and entertain. I know one group of women who go to do manicures. Most important of all, you can teach them the love of Jesus and how they can respond to that love. Sometimes family members of the nursing home patient become Christians. You get their attention when you care for their loved one.

Another area of work in benevolent ministries is comforting and caring for those who have lost a loved one. Many of us find this to be the hardest of times. One of my grandmother's greatest ministries was taking care of the kitchens at the homes of the recently bereaved. She could go into their kitchen and feel at home. She organized the food brought by friends and neighbors and marked all the containers to be returned. If they were short on an item, she would run to the grocery store and pick it up. She saw that everyone was fed. This took a heavy burden off the family members. It came to be that if there was a death in our little town, my grandmother was one of the first ones called and she was usually the first person to arrive at the home to offer help and condolences.

In my files, I have a list of do's and don'ts concerning offering condolences. They are very practical suggestions. They may be of help to you as you comfort those who have lost a loved one.

<u>Do's</u>
1. Do talk about the good times. Tell of a pleasant memory.
2. Do talk about the admirable traits of the deceased.

3. Do talk about the love shared.

4. Do be there even if you do not say one word.

6. Do check back on them in a couple of weeks.

Don'ts

1. Don't say, "I know how you feel." Even if you have had a similar loss, don't compare their pain with yours. If you truly know how they feel, they will know.

2. Don't say, "It was God's will." They may know that it is God's will, but at this time they do not want it to be.

3. Don't say, "She had a good long life." You hurt when you lose a dear loved one regardless of their age.

An area of benevolence that has been the hardest for me is when there is a dirty, disgusting job that needs doing. I have trouble with tasks such as cleaning a bathroom that hasn't been touched for some time, or cleaning up a mess made by animals or humans. I'll try if you don't mind me gagging all the way through. I would never have made a nurse, would I? I want to honor two women who have been so good at this. They are Virginia Bristol and Delores Bolte. Whatever you need done, they will do, and you never hear a complaint.

Caring for foster children is another area of benevolent care in which many in our congregation have been involved. Most were short term, but some of the families adopted these children. We cared for teenage girls who needed therapeutic care. There is a great need for families who will share their home with children who can't live in their own home any longer. At one time, we had six or eight families involved in this program. We were a help to each other as we cared for these children. We were known around town as the church that cared for needy children.

As Christians, we sometimes become discouraged in reaching out to others, especially if we see someone misusing the things provided or not being appreciative. Paul exhorts us: "Let us not become weary in doing good, for at the proper time we will reap a harvest if we do not give up" (Gal. 6:9).

If there is a benevolent program already going on in your church, consider if it would be a great ministry for you and get involved under its leadership. If there isn't one, approach your elders about the possibility of organizing one. Women have that special touch to be very effective in this ministry. Remember, it is not a ministry unless we are dependable and accountable. If you sometimes, when it is convenient and you feel like it, go to see a woman from your church in the hospital, that's good but it's not a ministry. It is a ministry if you have contacted the benevolent leader and placed your name on a list with other women to go to the hospital when your time comes up. Or it is a ministry if you have let your elders know that you are working in one of these areas. Why is it necessary to be accountable? So the leaders will know that everyone's needs are being met. This not only applies to visiting the sick, but also to all areas of benevolence such as the food and clothing room, the nursing home, and comforting the grieving. The whole church must work together to accomplish the work.

Tips for Making Hospital Visits Pleasant

1. Call the patient before you visit. Sometimes people are too sick to appreciate a visit. Usually there is a family member in her room who will answer the phone and instruct you concerning the visit. Sometimes, if the patient is very sick, there are family members in

the waiting room who would appreciate your visit and expression of concern for them and their sick loved one.

2. It is not necessary to take a gift, but a small token of love is always appreciated. My custom is to take one red rose. Also, a card or plant is a good idea. Some people take candy or gum when they know the patient is able to have them. The church bulletin, the newspaper, or a book or magazine are usually appreciated.

3. If you are visiting another woman who is a member of your church, ask if you can pray with her. The patient will find great comfort in your prayers going to the Father together. Hold her hand, and if there are other women with you, make a prayer circle. Be observant and make your prayer short if she is uncomfortable because of her illness.

4. Be a good listener. If she needs to, let her talk. Don't change the subject to talk about yourself unless she asks.

5. Ask if you can take care of needs at home while she is away. Volunteer to help with the kids, do the laundry, run errands, etc. It's a helpless feeling to be unable to take care of these things and you can take some of the stress from her by filling in.

6. Keep visits short unless you feel she needs your company. Don't be shy about asking if she would like for you to sit with her for a while. Otherwise, keep your visits to about five minutes. Very sick people appreciate your coming by, but sometimes do not feel up to chatting. Sometimes they do not like noise in the room. When my husband had his appendix taken out, friends came by and we had a blast laughing at funny stories, but the next day he was very sore and suffered much from the entertainment.

7. Do not bring up disturbing news, problems at church, or dangers of any kind. She does not need this. She has enough problems at the moment. Keep the conversation positive.

8. Do not visit when you are feeling down unless you can overcome that feeling and present a positive front. She does not need to know about your problems right now.

9. Call the women's ministry leader and let her know how the visit went. Are there needs that other women can be meeting? Will she be there long enough to merit another visit from one of the ladies? Does she need more help at home? The leader will enlist the necessary help. You, or the leader, will need to give a report to the person who types the church bulletin.

10. Continue to pray for the sick person. Send a card and let her know that you're praying for her. Call her when she is feeling better.

Discussion Questions

1. Is there a need for your services in the benevolent program at church? Is there a need to start one? What needs do you see?

2. List the areas of benevolence discussed in this chapter.

3. What blessings would come from this ministry?

4. How could this ministry be outreach?

5. How do you feel about being on the receiving end of acts of benevolence? On the giving end?

6. Give a Bible example of a benevolent woman.

7. Which benevolent ministry would you find hardest to accomplish? Which one would be easiest for you? Why?

8. Do you find it hard to minister to the bereaved? Have someone who has lost a loved one share what they appreciated from their church family.

9. Discuss a time when you were sick or hurting and a sister ministered to you. Discuss a time when you were sick and no one ministered to you. How did you feel?

10. Is this your ministry? Why or why not?

— NOTES —

CHAPTER EIGHT

Women in Ministries of Friend-to-Friend Counseling

Are you the woman in your church or community to whom everyone seems to come with their problems? Do you find yourself comforting someone at church when they have lost a loved one, listening to a friend about her marital problems, helping someone look through the want-ads for a job, helping sort through a conflict between two people, or encouraging a new Christian? If so, God has given you a special gift as your ministry. Many people prefer to discuss their problems with a friend, neighbor, or Christian sister than to go through the steps to consult a professional counselor.

All Christians should be counselors to some extent. We are all called to draw upon the resources of God— Scripture, prayer, church, and the Holy Spirit—to teach, lead, direct, and help others with their lives and problems. Although not professional counselors, some are more gifted at helping others in this area. Friend-to-friend or sister-to-sister counseling is sometimes the most effective.

A friend-to-friend counselor is a woman who helps another woman use God's resources in the same way she has learned to use them in her own life. She not only has learned God's teachings as principle, but has put them into practice. Paul says, "Follow my example as I follow the example of Christ" (1 Cor. 11:1). Luke says, "...everyone who is fully trained will be like his teacher" (Luke 6:40). Christ considered teaching to include much more than just communication of knowledge. The Scriptures state that His method was successful. Enemies recognized from their knowledge and behavior that the disciples had been with Jesus: "When they saw the courage of Peter and John and realized that they were unschooled, ordinary men, they were astonished and they took note that these men had been with Jesus" (Acts 4:13).

If you are a woman to whom other women come with problems, be careful that they are coming for the right reason. Are they coming for sound Biblical advice or for sympathy and enabling? You have failed if you are sympathetic toward explanations and excuses and do not hold your friend responsible for her behavior. Sympathy without confrontation can enable her to continue the inappropriate behavior. God has called us to give Biblical advice, tell the truth, help her face up to her own sins concerning the problem, and encourage her to make the changes necessary in her life. As a friend–to–friend counselor we must not become so emotionally involved that we, like our friend, can't see the problem clearly.

When a friend is trying to tell us of a sin, we should never minimize it by saying, "Well, you aren't any worse than anyone else. Everyone has sin in his or her life." Or, if a friend is trying to tell us she is sorry for something she has done to us or said about us, we should not say, "Oh, just forget about it. I have." Rather we should say, "Thank you for coming to me. I appreciate that you are doing this God's way. You are forgiven." In a ladies' class on commitment, one woman—a dear sister of seventy-something years—was in tears, trying to tell the class that she had not been committed to the Lord in the way she wanted to be. The sisters in class, trying to comfort her, were saying, "Oh, you have done more than all of us," or "You do so much, how can you feel this way?" The woman said, "No, let me finish, listen to me, I am confessing a sin and I plan to be a better person." What should the ladies have done? They should have said, "By rededicating your life and confessing your sins, you are a wonderful example to all of us. Thank you for sharing this with us."

Support groups have become very popular and seem to be effective in helping people deal with problems. Because they have been used in the secular world with success, the church has started to offer them also. Support groups bring together those with similar problems. In the group are people who have overcome, as well as those in the midst of, the problem. If you have had an experience in which you successfully worked through a difficult time in your life, you could be a great help in one of these groups. Support groups include: divorced women, widows, single women, working women, women who have husbands who do not come to church with them, and women who are caring for aging parents or sick family members. These groups need someone with good counseling skills to keep the atmosphere on a positive and constructive note.

I recommend a book to all friend-to-friend counselors. It is Gary Collins' book, "*How To Be A People Helper.*" Gary calls friend-to-friend counselors "people helpers," and he puts great confidence in their abilities:

> If you have ever had a friend help you through a crisis, you probably have concluded that peer counseling does work. But apart from our personal experiences, is there evidence that peer helping can be effective? A number of researchers have sought to answer this question, and their conclusions have been consistent. Paraprofessional or lay counselors generally are as effective as professional helpers. In a detailed book about lay counseling, Christian psychologist Siang-Yang Tan reviewed all of the research studies on the effectiveness of peer counseling. He acknowledged that there is still debate among professionals, but the overwhelming weight of evidence supports the conclusion that lay counselors frequently are as effective as professionals. There even is evidence that peer counselors often are better than professionals.

Collins goes on to say:

> One of my former professors was Dr. Joseph Matarazzo, a man who eventually became president of the American Psychological Association. After practicing psychotherapy and doing research for twenty-five years, my former teacher concluded that, except for a very small percentage of cases, like those involving people who are seriously disturbed by a severe life crisis or by immobilizing anxiety, most peer counselors are effective. What the majority of professional counselors accomplish in psychotherapy cannot be distinguished from what

is accomplished between very good friends over coffee
every morning in neighborhoods and in countless work
settings anywhere.

An effective friend-to-friend counselor must be full
of goodness and filled with knowledge: "I myself am
convinced, my brothers, that you yourselves are full
of goodness, complete in knowledge and competent to
instruct one another" (Rom. 15:14). As we grow as
Christians, we become full of goodness. It is one of the
Christian qualities listed in 2 Peter 1:5: "Make every effort
to add to your faith goodness; and to goodness,
knowledge..." Knowledge comes from being in the Word.
If we are not filled with knowledge of God's Word, we
will give secular counseling instead of godly counseling.

An effective friend-to-friend counselor must have a
rich knowledge of God's Word that develops wisdom:
"Let the word of Christ dwell in you richly as you
teach and counsel one another with all wisdom, and
as you sing psalms, hymns and spiritual songs with
gratitude in your hearts to God" (Col. 3:16). For the
word of God to dwell in you richly does not mean just
memorizing Biblical facts, but the application of
Scripture in your life. As we study the Word we gain
knowledge. As we gain knowledge, God gives us wisdom
to use it effectively.

An effective friend-to-friend counselor must be
willing for her life to be an example for others to follow.
Paul said, "Follow my example, as I follow the example
of Christ" (1 Cor. 11:1). We would not put much confidence
in someone who would tell us one thing and do another.
Much is written today concerning mentoring. A mentor
is someone who provides guidance and teaching by
their examples in everyday life. A mentor can be
someone who has agreed to the responsibility, or you

may choose a mentor without them even knowing it. When I think of the lady who taught me the gospel, I realize she taught me as much with her actions as with her words. The Bible gives us many examples of mentors. Naomi was a mentor for Ruth, Elizabeth for Mary and, most important of all, Jesus was a mentor for His disciples.

An effective friend-to-friend counselor must be a good listener. Have you ever had someone come to you and talk about a problem? When they get up to leave, they thank you for your help and you haven't done a thing except listen. Sometimes all they need is someone to listen. By voicing their problem aloud, they see a new perspective. Learning about active listening can help you be of help to others. In active listening, the helper restates what has been said using different words. This helps the person to see the problem in your words, and it helps her know that someone understands what she is trying to say.

An effective friend-to-friend counselor must be caring and loving: "We love because he first loved us. If anyone says, 'I love God,' yet hates his brother, he is a liar. For anyone who does not love his brother, whom he has seen, cannot love God, whom he has not seen" (1 John 4:19,20). People can tell very quickly if we have a genuine concern or if we just couldn't care less. If we do not have love, we are just going through the motions: "If I speak in the tongues of men and of angels, but have not love, I am only a resounding gong or a clanging cymbal" (1 Cor. 13: 1).

An effective friend-to-friend counselor must be willing to call people to repentance: "I have declared to both Jews and Greeks that they must turn to God in repentance and have faith in our Lord Jesus" (Acts 20:21). This is the hardest of all the qualifications for a people helper and the one we most often abuse. We have a tendency to make excuses, rationalize, and minimize sins in ourselves as well as others. We hesitate to talk to someone about their sin. We call it "minding our own business." We must not enable others to stay in their sin. An enabler cannot be an effective counselor.

An effective friend-to-friend counselor allows others to take responsibility for their own thoughts or actions. Do not minimize a sin someone is trying to confess. It's our human nature to comfort, but sometimes we comfort at the wrong time. Let them talk. Comfort later. Sometimes comforting too soon can stop the confession process that leads to changes: "Therefore, confess your sins to each other and pray for each other so that you may be healed. The prayer of a righteous man is powerful and effective" (James 5:16). Overprotective parents sometimes do not let their children take responsibility for their actions. They take the child's side in any situation. The other person is always the bad guy. If the teacher gives the child a bad grade, the teacher did not explain the subject well enough. If there is an argument among friends, my child is always right. We need to teach our children to take responsibility for their actions and deal with the consequences. We also need to let the people we are helping take responsibility for their actions.

An effective friend-to-friend counselor must know when to refer the person they are trying to help to someone with more experience and education. Sometimes people need more than we can give them. Their problems may be too complicated for us. We should be alert to this and refer them to a professional counselor who can help them. If friend-to-friend counseling is your ministry, have at your disposal a list of professionals to whom you can refer your helpees when you are not able to help. You should research the professional counselors in order to know the areas in which they are most known to be effective. I have known people who went to two or three counselors before finding one who could help. As friend-to-friend counselors we can help them avoid this problem.

As a friend-to-friend counselor, we must be willing to learn a few basic people-helping principles and counseling skills. There are many good books and mini-seminars to go to for help. When I was a foster parent, I learned much from seminars offered free through the Department of Human Services. I was surprised at what I did not know about people. Make it your business to educate yourself. You will be much more effective as a people helper.

Our main objective in people helping, or friend-to-friend counseling, is to help people change. Collins gives seven influencing skills to help people change:

(1) Restating, paraphrasing, summarizing. Here the helper pulls together what has been said and repeats or restates this using different words. This lets the helpee see the problem in a new light.

(2) Giving feedback. Sometimes there is a need for accurate data on how the helper or others view the person who has come for help. Try to be specific, nonjudgmental, and informative. Remember that most people can accept only one piece of information like this at a time, so don't overwhelm. Give the helpee opportunity to respond. For example: "Mary, I wonder if you have noticed that every time I begin to talk, you interrupt me. I suspect that others feel frustrated like I do when we aren't able to get a word in edgewise."

(3) Making self-disclosures. At times the helper expresses his or her thoughts or feelings to the helpee. It can be useful for the helpee to know how you are

feeling, but be careful not to shift the focus of helping onto yourself or imply that your attitudes, emotions, or opinions are the only valid or correct ones. It is best to start your self-disclosure by using statements like "From my perspective..." "I wonder if..." "It seems to me that..." or "Once I was in a somewhat similar situation when..."

(4) Making suggestions, giving advice, or providing information. Sometimes others need guidance, information, or skills that will help them deal with issues more effectively. It is best to be respectful and gentle in giving advice, guidance, information, or suggestions. Helpers often give advice without listening first. There is often a tendency to tell people what to do—especially when we aren't sure what else to say. In turn, the recipients of this information often resist being told how to change, and frequently such advice is ignored. Try, instead, to give information in the form of suggestions. For example, "How would you feel about talking directly to your boss about the way you are being treated?" or "I have some suggestions that might help you to study more effectively." Give the helpee opportunity to agree, disagree, or respond in other ways.

(5) Making interpretation. Here the helpee is given a different and unique way of looking at some issue. Be tentative as you present your interpretations of what is going on; you could be wrong. For example, "John, I noticed that most of the problems you have mentioned revolve around issues of authority. I wonder if these problems all show a tendency in you to resist any person who is in authority?"

(6) Stating logical consequences. This is a method by which the helper states what is likely to happen if the helpee continues on his or her present course of action. Once again, try not to use these statements as

hammers intended to force change. Words of manipulation almost always bring resistance. For example, instead of saying, "You had better cut this out or you're going to be on the street," it is usually better to say, "As you are smart enough to know, if this workaholic lifestyle persists, you could be successful in your career but lose your family." These statements of logical consequences can lead to discussions about how the helpee might change.

(7) Giving directives and making confrontations. This involves telling the helpee what he or she must do to change. Often this involves pointing out the inconsistencies, sinful relationships, or other attitudes and behaviors that need to be changed (49,50).

If you are a woman to whom people come with problems, you have a very special ministry. You are in great demand in the church. It will take courage and boldness to be all you can be in this area. It will take being in the Word daily to know the answers. It will take much love and caring. It will take praying to God for wisdom and relying on His Holy Spirit to lead you. Then, by the grace of God, strive to become the most effective you can be for God in your ministry.

Discussion Questions

1. Do women often come to you with problems? Why or why not?

2. List the qualification(s) you possess that make you an effective people helper.

3. List the qualification(s) you need to learn or improve in order to make you an effective people helper.

4. Why is it easy to sympathize and hard to confront?

5. List people who have influenced or mentored you in your Christian walk.

6. What support groups are needed in your church?

7. What do you feel would be the hardest part about being a people helper?

8. Discuss Gary Collins' seven influencing skills.

9. Look in your church library and list books available to help you be an effective people helper.

10. Is there a need in your church for more people helpers? Is this your ministry? Why or why not?

— NOTES —

❖ CHAPTER NINE ❖

Women in Ministries of Encouragement

Although we are all called to be givers of encouragement, some women have a special talent for encouraging. There is usually at least one major encouragement giver in every congregation. Sometimes it is a woman. Was she just born with that talent or did she develop it?

The Bible calls encouraging a gift. "If [a person's gift from God] is encouraging, let him encourage" (Rom.12:8). From this Scripture we see that people are given this gift from God. And what a gift it is. What would we do without these special people?

The Bible gives us an example of a man who was an encouragement giver: "Joseph, a Levite from Cyprus, whom the apostles called Barnabas (which means Son of Encouragement), sold a field he owned and brought the money and put it at the apostles' feet" (Acts 4:36,37). Why did the apostles call him Barnabas? It was probably because he was always encouraging. It would be nice if we were known as "daughters of encouragement." If a sister is feeling a little down, there should be a smile, a hug, a pat on the back, and words of encouragement waiting close by. One little lady of ninety-plus years encourages me every Sunday with a kiss and hug. That hug and kiss says, "It's good to see you and I care about you."

The encouragement giver is a positive person. She has as many problems as anyone else, but she doesn't let them get in the way of encouraging others. Recently I felt burdened by some problems in the life of one of my children. I was in the grocery store filling my cart with groceries, but deep in thought about the problems. A Christian sister, who was there also, interrupted my thoughts by saying, "What is up with you? I almost had to run my cart into yours to get you to acknowledge me." I apologized for being lost in my own little world. She knew about the problems. She smiled, sympathized, listened, hugged me, told me God loves me and so does she, and told me she has been praying daily for my family and me. She assured me we would get through the problem. She said, "With God's help you can get through anything." She quoted the Scripture: "I can do everything through Him who gives me strength" (Phil. 4:13). We talked for ten minutes about me and mine. She lifted my spirits. She gave me hope. As she left, she waved and smiled. Just before she rounded the corner of the aisle, she stopped and said, "I would appreciate you remembering me in your prayers. I lost my job today." Another wave and smile and she was gone. She had just reminded me of a marvelously beautiful truth. She knew who was in control of her life. She could be an encouragement to others even when things were not perfect in her own life. I thought of the apostle Paul. He encouraged others when his life was far from perfect. In prison, in chains, he wrote: "And my God will meet all your needs according to his glorious riches in Christ Jesus" (Phil. 4:19). His thoughts were on others even when his life was less than perfect. Dale Galloway, in his book *12 Ways to Develop a Positive Attitude*, has this to say: "Practice the principle of replacement. For every negative emotion, there's a positive emotion that can be selected by you to eliminate the negative one. Replace: anger with love; fear with faith; despair with hope; greed with generosity; sorrow with joy; complaint with gratitude; worry with trust; guilt with forgiveness" (36). The encouragement givers among us have learned this lesson.

The encouragement giver looks for the good in circumstances and people. This does not mean we "bury our heads in the sand" where negative things are concerned. We do not refuse to recognize the negative, but we refuse to dwell on it. Recently I was teaching my grandson that we must be truthful—but tactful—where people's feelings are concerned. I told him you can always find something good to say in any circumstance. He said, "What if a woman asks you if her dress is pretty and you hate it?" I told him to find something about the dress that is pretty—maybe a color in the material, or the collar. Later in church he asked me if I liked a dress a lady was wearing. I said, "Not especially, why?" He said, "It's a pretty color, isn't it?" He was testing me to see if I practiced what I taught. We must see the good in others. There is good in the worst sinner. There is good in the person who creates a negative atmosphere. There is good in the person with the bad attitude. Encouragement givers look for the good in people and circumstances.

The giver of encouragement is the first one to acknowledge and compliment the good things people have done. We sometimes treat our Christian sisters as we have a tendency to treat our children. We reinforce negative behavior by giving consequences, but forget to reinforce positive behavior with words of encouragement. While we are called to confront and help correct negative behavior in our sisters, we should be just as quick to compliment jobs well done. Encouragement is a basic human need. We have far too many people who try to tell us we can't do it, or that we should be realistic, or that we have our heads in the clouds. Sometimes this is said with attitudes and not words. Sometimes this is said by not saying anything, but by being silent. Our perspective of their silence is "they did not approve." All of us love to hear words of acknowledgment. We all know this but the encouragement giver really "knows" this.

When I was in high school, I was always the one elected to be the secretary to take the minutes or the reporter to write the events for the newspaper. My classmates would say, "Let's elect Pam because she has a way with words." Although I was very insecure, this encouragement was probably the first thing that put into my heart the desire to write. Those words, "she has a way with words," stayed in my mind. Encouraging words are like that. The person receiving them remembers long after the person saying them has forgotten.

Encouragement givers are quick to give recognition. This is completely biblical. Paul brings this out in many of his letters: "I was glad when Stephanas, Fortunatus and Achaicus arrived, because they have supplied what was lacking from you. For they refreshed my spirit and yours also. Such men deserve recognition" (1 Cor. 16:17,18). Again Paul, speaking of Epaphroditus, says to the Christians at Philippi: "Welcome him in the Lord with great joy, and honor men like him, because he almost died for the work of Christ, risking his life to make up for the help you could not give me" (Phil. 2:29,30). To the church at Rome he said: "Be devoted to one another in brotherly love. Honor one another above yourselves" (Rom. 12:10). His admonition to Timothy was: "The elders who direct the affairs of the church well are worthy of double honor, especially those whose work is preaching and teaching" (1 Tim. 5:17). A preacher or elder will be more effective in his job if he is appreciated, honored, and recognized by the members for his hard work. A woman will be more effective in her ministry if recognition is shown.

I have heard all sorts of excuses why we do not show recognition. I have heard, "It will cause them to be puffed up," and "We are not to honor anyone but Christ." Well, Paul must not have known this. He freely gave honor and recognition, and he encouraged those to whom he was writing to do the same.

An encouragement giver corrects gently. The encouragement giver knows that everyone makes mistakes or fails at one time or another. When my husband was a young Christian, he was eager to be involved in everything at church. The older men's leadership, the song leaders, the preacher, and those who led the prayers intrigued him. Finally, the time came and he was asked to lead a prayer. He led a beautiful prayer straight from his heart. Afterwards, a dear sister who had a big part in our conversions talked with us. She told him what a great job he had done and how proud she was of him. She told him God had great things in store for him. Then she said, "There is one thing I would like to call to your attention. You prayed that God would bless this beautiful Sabbath day. The Sabbath Day is Saturday. Sunday is the Lord's

Day, the first day of the week." She went on to explain the difference. We never forgot that lesson but most of all we never forgot the sweet and gentle way in which she taught it. This could have been devastating to a young Christian if done in an improper way. For example, it could have been devastating if someone had laughingly said, "Don't you know the difference between the Sabbath and Sunday?"

As encouragement givers, we must remember that mistakes and failures are only the stepping stones of life. Look at the example of Abraham Lincoln. He failed in business in 1831. He was defeated for the legislature in 1832. He was elected to the legislature in 1834. His sweetheart died in 1835. He had a nervous breakdown in 1836. He was defeated for speaker in 1838. He was defeated for elector in 1840. He was defeated for Congress in 1843. He was elected to Congress in 1846. He was defeated for Congress in 1848. He was defeated for Senate in 1850. He was defeated for vice president in 1856. He was defeated for Senate in 1858. But, he was elected president of the United States in 1860. He must have had some great encouragement givers in his life.

A young woman in public speaking class received an "F" on her first speech and determined to never try again. "It's not my ministry," she said. "I am too shy." Later in another class she tried again. The wise teacher encouraged her and directed her toward a subject that would help her with her fears. She tried again and, to the amazement of her classmates, did a great job. The Word says, "...Encourage the timid..." (1 Thess. 5:14). "For God did not give us a spirit of timidity, but a spirit of power, of love and of self discipline" (2 Tim. 1:7).

One of the ways I've seen women encourage other women the most is when they are open about their lives. Personal stories of problems and how they were overcome in godly ways are very beneficial for encouraging others with the same problems. It gives them hope. It's the "if you were delivered and overcame, then I can, too" attitude. After all, "Nothing in all creation is hidden from God's sight. Everything is uncovered and laid bare before the eyes of him to whom we must give account" (Heb. 4:13). The words laid bare mean total transparency. God knows everything about us. If we can become more transparent with our sisters in Christ, we can give much encouragement. Women of my generation tend to be more private. There are things in our pasts that we have overcome with God's help that we would just as soon not tell you about. We have been forgiven and as far as we—and God—are concerned, they no longer exist. If I tell of a problem in my past that I overcame, I might start with the words, "I knew a woman once who..." I see my daughters exhibiting a different mindset. Their generation of Christian sisters is much more transparent. They share openly about problems and how God helped them overcome the problems. Women need this openness. Many are laden with poor self-esteem, guilt, or fear because of sins in their pasts. This sometimes causes physical, spiritual, or emotional sickness. When we share our victories, they are more apt to share also. One woman told me she had felt guilty all her adult life because of a past sin. She was able to release the guilt, with the help of reassurances by the women in her study group, because they loved her regardless of her past. She found out she was "no worse" than anyone else; that all had sinned. Women can't be effective in the kingdom if they are guilt laden. When they share with us, and see we love them and care for them anyway, they can understand how God can love them anyway. As encouragement givers, we reinforce their self-worth and their God-worth. There is a danger in being transparent. We must be completely remorseful about past sins. When we asked one young woman why she started drinking alcohol, her reply was, "When our youth director shared that he drank alcohol in the past, he made it sound like so much fun." God forbid!

I would like to see our churches adopt an idea used in the business world that helps encourage. I was a home interior displayer for a few years earlier in my life. Once a week I attended a sales meeting where successful displayers told their stories of how they accomplished the high sales for the week. They had great ideas that worked. Their story was "if I can do it, you can, too." It worked. I know, because when I did what they did, I was successful also. And I had a few good ideas of my own to share. In the church, I would like to hear more Christians tell where they have been and what happened in their lives to get them to where they are now. It can be very encouraging to the weak Christian to hear what it took for growth. We look around in our assemblies and we feel that all these people were just raised in the church, became Christians, and have always been strong. This isn't true. There are many success stories of how we defeated Satan, and I would like to hear us sharing them.

There is a great way to give encouragement that can be done by anyone, from the most active church member to someone who is restricted by health or distance. It can be done from your own home. It can be done from your favorite chair. (This is also covered under literary ministries.) If it is your ministry, you should take it seriously. It is encouragement written by you and mailed. You can cover everyone and everything with this ministry. It requires an ample supply of note pads, stationery, prayer grams, appreciate-a-grams, cards, and postage stamps. Mail notes to new people at church, people asking for prayers, the sick and discouraged, those who have failed, those who have been criticized or rejected by someone, and those you can compliment or otherwise recognize. Little notes have opened many hearts for later having the opportunity to share the Gospel. I once asked some new members at our church how it happened that they started coming. They said, "Well, we visited four or five churches and no one seem to care until we came to your church. After our first visit, we received eight cards telling us that they were glad we visited and to please come again." Purchase your local newspaper and send notes of congratulations to those getting married, celebrating anniversaries, and being honored. Send condolences to those who have lost loved ones in death. Doors can open from little notes of love.

We should be encouragement givers in the area of spiritual growth. Maybe we have found our ministry and we are hard at work in the kingdom. But many women have not. When we see a woman stepping out to try something new, such as teaching a class, we should be there to encourage her. We can back her up. A first-time teacher usually welcomes this. We may think we can learn more in the class of an experienced teacher and choose it over the less experienced. But where can we be the best at encouraging? The new teacher needs us.

As a teacher of women at the Bear Valley Bible Institute, I am constantly faced with the job of encouraging young women. They are preparing to be preachers' wives and missionaries' wives. They are sometimes fearful of what lies ahead. Words of encouragement from someone who has been in the field go a long way. I challenge them to examine their interests, talents, and hobbies in order to determine their talents for serving in the church. I challenge them to step out on faith to use their talents, knowing that God will bless them with more and more talents (Matt. 25:14-30). I encourage them when growth is shown in new areas.

Several Scriptures tell us to encourage one another daily: "But encourage one another daily, as long as it is called Today, so that none of you may be hardened by sin's deceitfulness" (Heb. 3:13). "Let us not give up meeting together, as some are in the habit of doing, but let us encourage one another—and all the more as you see the Day approaching" (Heb. 10:25). As encouragement givers, we could make a plan to call someone on the phone every day for the sole purpose of encouraging with positive words of love and caring. In a few short minutes, we could make a big impact in someone's life.

It is best to have an organized encouragement committee. People have the best intentions to get the cards, notes, and phone calls out, but many times do not follow through. The young woman received the eight cards after she had visited the church because of an organized ministry. It did not just happen. Is directing this committee your ministry? Is being involved in this committee your ministry? If your church has a women's ministry leader, consult her about an encouragement committee. If your church does not have a women's ministry leader, consult your elders about starting an encouragement committee. If there is no plan by either of them, make it your personal ministry and encourage a few other women to join you in this ministry.

Encouragement is a much-needed ministry. Remember, to be a ministry, it must be consistent. It cannot be something that you hit-and-miss once in a while when you feel like it. It is a great ministry, but will require your time and planning. It will require being observant of needs. It is best to have a certain day, or time of day, that you plan to devote to this ministry. Monday morning is a great time to sit down with your church bulletin and announcements from Sunday morning and write your notes of encouragement. Encouragement givers can open doors for the Gospel that no one else has managed to do. Is this your ministry?

Discussion Questions

1. Are you an encouragement giver, or do you take it for granted that people know how you feel without you saying anything?

2. How much of your time would it take to make this your ministry?

3. List names of encouragement givers in your congregation. In what ways do they encourage you and others?

4. How do you feel about women encouraging women through sharing personal triumphs?

5. Discuss ways to encourage.

6. Why are we sometimes slow to give compliments and recognition?

7. How can we encourage the timid?

8. What ways are you already showing encouragement?

9. How can we encourage one another daily? Give Scriptures that tell us to do this.

10. Discuss encouraging women to use their talents. How have you been encouraged in this area?

❖ CHAPTER TEN ❖

Women in Ministries with the Aging

People over the age of sixty-five constitute a large percentage of the membership in the church today. This is one of the fastest-growing groups in our country, yet, most of the church's emphasis and activities center around younger people.

Every church needs someone to work with the aging, someone who will help engage their talents, energy, time, and wisdom. Someone is needed not only to see that this group of people is being seen to amidst the day-to-day problems that arise, but also to help them be productive in the kingdom. They need a supportive atmosphere in which to share their concerns, strengths, abilities, and talents. Although the aged person may have slowed down from younger years, they still have much to give and can remain very effective in the kingdom.

What should be the requirements of the person who would work with these people? It would require a person who is caring and sensitive to the experiences of growing older. It would require a person who is supportive and provides an atmosphere in which the elderly can share their concerns, strengths, and abilities, and develop their talents. It might require that you become more familiar with subjects concerning the elderly—such as retirement, grief, bereavement, and crisis intervention—in order to be more effective in your ministry.

We sometimes do not take advantage of the wisdom and expertise found in this group of people. They have much to offer. There is no greater source of instruction and encouragement for younger women than the wisdom of an older woman: "Gray hair is a crown of splendor; it is attained by a righteous life" (Prov. 16:31). We all know a sweet little gray-haired lady who radiates the joy of the Lord. She has walked with him for years and it shows in her countenance: "Who is like the wise man? Who knows the explanation of things? Wisdom brightens a man's face and changes its hard appearance" (Ecclesiastes 8:1). We can learn from her if we will only take the time to stop and listen. Many times we hurry back and forth, in and out, all around the wise older women as we look for answers and solutions. She sits, waiting for us to notice. She knows she can help. We come near but do not stop. She bows her head in sadness knowing she could help if given a chance.

We have many Bible examples of people being effective for God at an older age. Abraham and Sarah laughed when, in their old age, God revealed His plan for them to have a child:

> God also said to Abraham, "As for Sarai your wife, you are no longer to call her Sarai; her name will be Sarah. I will bless her and will surely give you a son by

her. I will bless her so that she will be the mother of
nations; kings of peoples will come from her." Abraham
fell facedown; he laughed and said to himself, "Will a
son be born to a man a hundred years old? Will Sarah
bear a child at the age of ninety" (Gen. 17:15-17)?

The renaming of Sarah stressed that she was to be
the mother of nations and kings and that she would
serve the Lord's purpose.

Another Bible example of a person being effective
at an older age is Moses. He was not a young man
when he was called from tending the flocks to become
the shepherd of God's people. You know the story of
how he spent his growing-up years in the palace of
Pharaoh. When he was grown, he tried to help the
Hebrew people in their hardships. Because of an incident
that happened, he was afraid and ran away. He was
forty years old when he went to the land of Midian.
"When Moses was forty years old, he decided to visit
his fellow Israelites. He saw one of them being
mistreated by an Egyptian, so he went to his defense
and avenged him by killing the Egyptian. Moses thought
that his own people would realize that God was using
him to rescue them, but they did not" (Acts 7:23-25).
After escaping to Midian, he married, had a son, and
spent a long period of time there. "Moses agreed to stay
with the man, who gave his daughter Zipporah to Moses
in marriage. Zipporah gave birth to a son, and Moses
named him Gershom, saying, 'I have become an alien
in a foreign land'" (Ex. 2:21,22). Life was good for Moses
and his little family. He spent his days tending the flocks
and his nights around the fire with his family. He must
have thought he would live out his life there. But God
had other plans: "During that long period, the king of
Egypt died. The Israelites groaned in their slavery and

cried out, and their cry for help because of their slavery went up to God" (Exodus 21:23). That's when God decided that Moses, although older in years, would be the one to lead the Israelites out of Egypt. Moses was reluctant, but God's will for his life had to be accomplished. Would we have chosen Moses or a spirited younger man?

Remember how old Noah was when he built the ark? "Noah was six hundred years old when the floodwaters came on the earth" (Gen. 7:6). In the New Testament we might assume that Dorcas (Tabitha), the woman who died and was raised to life by Peter, was an older person because she kept company with other widows: "...All the widows stood around him, crying and showing him the robes and other clothing that Dorcas had made while she was still with them" (Acts 9:39).

For years Lloyd and Connie Roundy, of Council Bluffs, Iowa, have organized and directed the concerns and activities of the people in their older years. They work under the oversight of an elder. They call themselves the "Young at Hearts." If a woman chooses this as her ministry, I see no reason why she couldn't organize and carry it out, providing she works under the oversight of an elder, and providing she stays in her role of authority. If there is a problem in your church with a woman having this oversight, don't despair. Work with the widows. We had a group of widows who called themselves "The Golden Girls" after the television program, although that is the only thing they had in common.

An example of a woman who works with widows and older women is Mary Jane Kennon in McCrory, Arkansas. Her ministry involves teaching a ladies' Bible class, organizing a party once a month to celebrate birthdays, being available to listen to their problems on the phone, transporting them to the doctor when a family member isn't available, and many other opportunities. Is she sometimes taken for granted? Yes. Is she sometimes taken advantage of by others? Yes. But remember, this is her ministry to the Lord. While serving others, she is serving God.

The Bible is clear that we are to look after the needs of this group of people: "Religion that God our Father accepts as pure and faultless is this: to look after orphans and widows in their distress and to keep oneself from being polluted by the world" (James 1:27). We can also find instruction as to how this is to be done. In the book of Acts we find widows being overlooked in the daily distribution of food. The apostles, feeling their ministry was teaching the Word of God, knew they must appoint someone to see to these needs:

> "Brothers, choose seven men from among you who are known to be full of the Spirit and wisdom. We will turn this responsibility over to them and will give our attention to prayer and the ministry of the word."
>
> This proposal pleased the whole group. They chose Stephen, a man full of faith and of the Holy Spirit; also Philip, Prochorus, Nicanor, Timon, Parmenas, and Nicolas from Antioch, a convert to Judaism (Acts 6:3-5).

Although women are not mentioned in this Scripture, it is my guess that they were heavily involved in the preparation and distribution of the food to the widows.

Two Avenues to Take in this Ministry

I. Work on an individual basis. Make the elderly your personal ministry.

A. In our busy world, sometimes we don't take time to be there for them. Even family members of the elderly who have the best intentions find it hard to spend enough time with them.

1. They need someone to be there and give them undivided attention, even if it's just for five minutes.

2. They need someone to just listen.

3. They need someone to help them make today count.

B. Help each person you work with to find their place in the church. Everyone needs to be a part and feel they are essential.

1. Organize a telephone club for encouragement and to keep each other informed on how everyone is doing and on needs that arise.

2. Help them choose a young person or a young couple to help and encourage. Use the Titus 2 principle. The older women should teach and train the younger women.

3. Help them start a card ministry. Sending cards and notes of encouragement to the sick, visitors to church, etc., is a great

service opportunity. They can do this even on the coldest winter day from their favorite chair.

4. Encourage them to never stop sharing the Gospel with other people—even if it's over the phone or in written form—and to always have an evangelistic attitude. My little mom is 73 years old. When the preacher asked who in the congregation was going to share the Gospel with someone in the coming new year, she raised her hand. I was very proud of her.

5. Encourage them to always have a caring attitude.

6. Encourage them to use their talents in the church as long as they are physically and emotionally able. Who knows? They might be another Abraham or Sarah.

7. Remember their birthdays and send a card.

II. Organize a Program

A. Work under the leadership of an elder.

B. Invite other members of the church to be involved with you.

C. Invite guest speakers to help the group with subjects of concern such as health issues, dealing with grief, etc.

D. Keep the group in the Word.

134 ❖ Evangelistic Women

E. Organize activities: visit interesting places, do interesting things.

F. Organize a group to visit the nursing home for devotionals and encouragement.

G. Provide services and educational programs that will keep older people integrated into the mainstream of the church.

H. Celebrate birthdays with a party once a month.

I. Develop a bulletin board especially for them. On it should be announcements of events, news items, birthdays, etc.

J. Make plans for holidays for those who are alone.

A ministry with the aging is very rewarding, both to the one doing the ministering and to the recipients. This ministry can put your creative skills to work and keep you as busy as you care to be in the kingdom.

Discussion Questions

1. Why would you want to make working with the aging your ministry?

2.. What strengths and talents has God given you to make working with the aging your ministry?

3. Is there a need in your congregation for this ministry? If there is already a ministry with the aging, is there a need for your assistance in this ministry?

4. What do you see as the most pressing area of concern? What needs to be accomplished first?

5. What does the Bible say about our need to care for the aging?

6. Name Bible people who accomplished great things for the Lord in their older years.

7. How can we more effectively utilize the talents of our older people?

8. Give an example of an older lady who is busy doing the Lord's work.

9. This week, make an appointment with an older woman. Have her tell you her life's story. You may be surprised at the lessons she reveals.

10. What other thoughts do you have concerning this ministry?

— NOTES —

CHAPTER ELEVEN

Women in Organizational Ministries: Special Events

Special events are an important part of a church's activities. They are fun, festive occasions. However, they must have a purpose also. The purpose must always be to glorify God. Special events promote fellowship among the members and provide a warm, friendly atmosphere for guests. They are excellent public relations opportunities for the church. The fellowship at a special event can lead to a Bible study with the guest you invited. In this way, special events can be used as an evangelistic tool.

Many women have great organizational skills. They are very effective at planning and carrying out special events. We must use these talents in the church. It is a waste for women to only use these talents at their bridge clubs, or their children's school activities. A woman who is skilled at organizing, planning, and delegating can turn an enormous job into a smooth, fun activity where people love working together to accomplish a purpose.

Martha spent days planning a mother-daughter luncheon for the ladies at church. She first consulted the church office to receive authorization from the elders and to enter the event on the church calendar. Next, she secured a beautiful Victorian mansion, an appropriate setting for a ladies' fellowship. She negotiated the fee for the use of the mansion, arranged for the food with the manager, and met with the chefs to go over the details. Decorations and table settings were available at the mansion. She asked the church's secretary to run an announcement in the bulletin. She provided a place for women to sign up to determine the number of women who would attend. Then she formed a committee to plan an interesting program for the guests' enjoyment and encouragement.

Ann invited her friend Judy to the luncheon. They both took their daughters and the four of them enjoyed each other's company and the fellowship of the other women who were sitting at their table. The lunch and program that followed provided a memorable mother-daughter outing. During dinner, Judy and her daughter met several women from church. They found they had many things in common. Friendships began. On the way home, Judy asked Ann several questions about the church. She expressed interest in enrolling her daughter in Sunday Bible Class. Ann could see where God was leading this friendship. Soon she had the opportunity to study the Word with Judy, and she became a Christian. Following the luncheon, Martha heard many women voice their gratitude and thanks for the beautiful occasion, but the story that pleased her the most was Ann and Judy's story. She praised God that the luncheon was used to reach out to other people. The luncheon had been a success. God was glorified through Christian fellowship and outreach.

If Martha had chosen to have the luncheon at the fellowship hall at church, she would have needed several additional committees. Following is a list of committees necessary for a successful function:

1. Planning committee. This committee determines the purpose of the function. It decides on a theme. It recruits others to be heads of committees. It meets with all the other committees to assure that the theme is carried out successfully.

2. Preparing the fellowship hall committee. This committee makes sure the hall is clean, neat, and ready for the function. This is important because many people use the fellowship hall and it may not have been cleaned properly after the last function.

3. Promotion committee. This committee promotes the event through the church's bulletin, posters, etc. It takes the details of the event to the local newspaper to accept free public relations advertisement. The people in the community become aware of the church's activities. They see a church on the go, reaching out and doing something. Many churches do not take advantage of free advertisement.

4. Decorating committee. This committee provides the setting for the occasions. They are in charge of the scenery, tables, table coverings, table decorations, napkins, plates, and programs. They must be in touch with the food committee to provide appropriate table settings. They are also in charge of decorating any bulletin boards located in the fellowship hall. The bulletin boards should be decorated to match the theme of the party.

5. Food committee. This committee decides what will be served and how it will be served. It decides if the food will be catered, if the women will provide the food, or if there will be chefs from the congregations.

6. **Program committee.** This committee decides on a program that matches the function. It recruits people to lead or sing songs, decides who will offer the prayers, and acquires a speaker if one is needed. It decides if there will be testimonies, skits, or other activities.

7. **Clean-up committee.** This committee is a group of people who have agreed to stay until the last crumb is cleaned up and the last chair is back in place.

Some churches have a special event at least once a month. Following are a few suggestions:

January—Plan a New Year's celebration. It is not necessary that this event be on New Year's day. It can be on any day in January. Enjoy making New Year's resolutions together.

February—Plan a sweetheart banquet to promote the renewing of romance in marriages. (See suggestions at the end of this chapter.)

March—Plan a concert and ask a music group to entertain.

April—Plan a marriage retreat.

May—Plan a mother-daughter tea, picnic, luncheon, or banquet. (See suggestions at the end of this chapter.)

June—Help your husband plan an outing for fathers and sons.

July—Plan a picnic for Independence Day. Plan a Vacation Bible School.

August—Plan a back-to-school party for families.

September—Plan a Labor Day picnic.

October—Plan a talent show and involve as many people as possible. You may need to provide some of the skits, songs, and comedies to get people involved.

November—Plan a program to honor a special person. (See suggestions at the end of this chapter.) Plan a Thanksgiving dinner celebration.

December—Plan a festive holiday party.

Sweetheart Banquet and Program

Purpose

To create a fun night, filled with good food, good fellowship, and a time of renewing the special relationship between husbands and wives.

Theme

"Let Me Call You Sweetheart." The theme should be carried out in several places. It should be written on a large banner behind the Master of Ceremonies' table. It should be the title on the programs. The music to the song "Let Me Call You Sweetheart" should be playing as the guests arrive.

Decorations

Red and white are the most striking colors for February. The colors may be carried out in the table coverings, napkins, and dishes. Red valentine hearts add a special touch. Your fellowship hall or banquet hall should be decorated as festively as possible; it sets the mood for your entire evening.

Food

The organizer should select the menu.

Drinks

Nonalcoholic strawberry daiquiris make a beautiful drink. Red fruit punch or strawberry sherbet mixed with ginger ale can carry out your colors.

Program

Activity—As guests arrive, each one is given a bright red stick-on heart to wear. They are given a word they must not say. If they are caught saying the word, they lose their heart. You will hear dinner conversation about, "taking care of my heart" and "you just want my heart." The person with the most hearts at the end of the program wins a prize. As different people lose their heart, you will know about it from the commotion at their table as they give it up. Choose a common word to be used. We have used the word "no."

Welcome—The Master of Ceremonies gives welcoming remarks, introduces guests, etc.

Prayer—Always have a prayer before the meal.

Dinner—Enjoy the dinner and the heart game. As some are finishing their dinner, the organizer and her husband go from table to table meeting guests and helping everyone feel welcome.

Song—Have someone sing the theme song "Let Me Call You Sweetheart." A quartet would be great also.

Sweetheart stories—The core of the program consists of each couple standing together and telling their favorite sweetheart story. It can be told by the husband or wife, or by both together. It does not have to be about their courtship, marriage, or wedding day, although it can be. Any special event or special thing one has done for the other is great. It will add to the enjoyment of the occasion if some of the stories are funny. It is best to let the couples know in advance to bring their stories, or have a few designated to get the stories started. Decide on the favorite story by secret vote or applause. Honor the couple who told the best sweetheart story with a gift. If you have a large crowd, set a time limit for each story.

Photographs—Have a photographer available and a place decorated for a background for the pictures. Couples will be glad to pay a small fee for the keepsake picture.

Mother-Daughter Banquet and Program

Purpose

To create a special memory for mothers and daughters through a precious sharing time together. To help each woman realize her own special beauty and self-worth. To show the real beauty of a woman who lives for God.

Theme

"Oh! You Beautiful Doll," or "You Are Beautiful."

Decorations

Place a large sign behind the speaker's table with the words "Oh! You Beautiful Doll." Make your programs and name tags in the shape of a paper doll. Gather dolls from your friends, or from your friends' children. Grown-up dolls, Barbie dolls, and baby dolls will work. Arrange them on your tables as centerpieces.

Food

The organizer will select the menu.

Program:

Welcome—The Mistress of Ceremonies welcomes everyone, gives opening remarks, and makes introductions of visitors and program participants. Have those who brought guests stand and introduce their guests. Give each guest a red rose with a tag attached with the words, "You are beautiful."

Prayer—Always start with prayer.

Dinner—Enjoy the food and fellowship. As some are finishing their dinner, the organizer visits from table to table to greet guests and helps everyone feel welcome.

Songs—Have someone sing your theme song, or have a male quartet come in at this time to sing to the women.

Special Treat—Find someone who has a doll collection. A lady in our church had a beautiful collection. Some were very expensive, some were antiques, and some were just ordinary dolls. We set up a table for her to display her collection. She told us about each doll, where it was purchased, and the value of it. The young daughters at the banquet especially enjoyed this part of the program. The oldest of the group enjoyed it, too. Women never outgrow dolls. If you do not have anyone with a doll collection, have those who attend bring a doll. It could be one from their childhood, or one of their daughter's dolls. Have each woman tell about her doll.

Devotional—"Real Beauty"

The world puts great value on beauty. Every year "People Magazine" runs a special edition consisting of the ten most beautiful women in the world. Health and exercise clubs all over the world offer programs to make us beautiful. The cosmetic industry researches and markets billions of dollars in products for what the world calls external beauty.

An amount of all this is used by the Christian woman. The worthy woman in Proverbs 31:21,22 loved beautiful things. She made her clothing from fine linen and purple. Queen Esther, in the Old Testament, used her beauty to advance God's cause. She had come to royal position because of her great beauty. She used her position to help God's people. God is concerned with how we take care of our body. 1 Corinthians 3:16 says: "Don't you know that you yourselves are God's temple and that God's Spirit lives in you? If anyone destroys God's temple, God will destroy him; for God's temple is sacred, and you are that temple."

We can see there is some merit in taking care of ourselves externally, but there is a much greater beauty. Our focus should be upon internal beauty, the beauty of the soul.

How do we become beautiful? How do we develop internal beauty that reflects in everything we do? Romans 10:15 speaks of the person who brings the good news about Jesus as having beautiful feet. 1 Peter 3:4 speaks of the unfading beauty of a gentle and quiet spirit. A woman becomes truly beautiful only when she has completely given herself to her Lord and Master. The Holy Spirit is able to do His great work. Galatians 5:22-24 lists the fruit of the Spirit. As we mature in our Christian walk, we grow in love, joy, peace, patience, kindness, goodness, faithfulness, gentleness, and self-control. Colossians 3:12-14 tells us to clothe ourselves with compassion, kindness, humility, gentleness, patience, and love.

James 1:22,23 tells us to listen to the Word and do it. It says if we listen to the Word and do not do it, we are like the man who looks at his face in a mirror and then goes away and forgets what he looks like. We would not look into a mirror, see a flaw, and not try to correct it. Neither should we look into our spiritual mirror, see a flaw, and not correct it.

2 Corinthians 4:16 says: "But though our outward man perish yet the inward man is renewed day by day." The most beautiful woman in the world is the one who has walked hand in hand with God, served Him, and loved Him all the days of her life and is looking forward with great anticipation to being with Him in heaven. This woman truly glows with beauty.

To God Be the Glory

Purpose

To show honor to an individual for an accomplishment, or to celebrate a special birthday.

Theme

"To God Be The Glory." The theme will be carried out on a banner, the napkins, and in various other places in the program. The theme is to give God the glory for accomplishments, or birthdays.

Decorations

Use the honoree's favorite colors.

Food

A menu of your choice.

Program

Special Music—Have someone sing the honoree's favorite song or songs.

A Dozen Roses—The Master of Ceremonies gives introductory remarks about the person being honored. God is given the glory for the accomplishments, the person's life, etc. He explains the dozen roses. One person, or a group of people, will present one rose at a time to the honoree. The people presenting the roses may include: the children of the honoree, grandchildren of the honoree, a few friends representing the many friends of the honoree, the preacher from the honoree's church, the honoree's boss or ex-boss, the president or a representative of various clubs and organizations to which the honoree belongs, and any other representatives of the honoree's interests and activities. When each person comes forward, he or she will have a few words to say concerning the part of the honoree's life they are representing. They will present the honoree with one rose. When the program is completed, the honoree will be holding a dozen beautiful roses.

Video—A video presentation of the honoree's life, with pictures and special music, can be made in advance and is shown for all to enjoy.

Discussion Questions

1. List the purposes for having special events.

2. How can a special event be an evangelistic tool?

3. What story pleased Martha the most?

4. List seven necessary committees for having a special event.

5. With which committee do you usually work? Why?

6. List your qualifications for organizing special events.

7. What rewards come to the organizer of special events?

8. Make a list of special events your church could plan.

9. List women in the church who organize special events. Invite one of them to speak to your class concerning successes and failures.

10. Discuss using one of the special events in this chapter at the church you attend.

— NOTES —

CHAPTER TWELVE

Other Ministries for Women

Women in Missions Ministries

Are you a woman without many obligations at home? Maybe you have never been married, or maybe you are a widow with grown children. Are you the adventurous type ready to see the world and save the people? If so, your ministry may be missionary work.

Congregations are more open to sending women to the mission field than they were in past years. Elderships have seen the proof that women can be very useful and effective in the field just as they are in the home congregation.

The majority of women in missions are there with their husbands. I have never lived in the mission field, unless we can count Iowa, and maybe we should count Iowa since we were the only Church of Christ in Iowa within fifty miles. I have also gone on many campaigns in foreign countries with my husband, including England, Germany, Russia, and Canada.

My husband and I attended a World Mission Seminar at the Webb Chapel Church of Christ in Dallas, Texas. One of the ladies' classes was a brainstorming session concerning the role of women in missions in the local congregation and the role of women in missions in the field. Several of the things listed below were discussed in that session. A woman can be involved in missions either at the home congregation or in the field. Let's take a look at how we can be effective.

In the local church, there is need for someone to promote the mission effort. This can be done through articles written for the bulletin, newsletters, bulletin boards, Sunday school class awareness, banners, and sending supplies to missionaries. Also, articles may be written for the local paper.

Sending and grading Bible correspondence courses is a needed part of the missions ministry. World Bible School has letters from people all over the world asking for correspondence courses. Many churches are involved with them in this work. It helps a church become more aware of evangelism outside the local congregation. It gives a broader view of the church and its work. Prepare a special bulletin board with a world map. Place a marker at all the places where the local World Bible School group has students. I have seen women who had not found their ministry until they got involved as a teacher in World Bible School. The group meets to grade papers together. They share pictures and stories of their students.

The role of women in missions in the field would be much like the role of women in missions in any congregation. The same Scriptures apply concerning taking care of the home and teaching and training women. Personally, when I spent three weeks in Russia, I taught classes from eight to five and did public relations work with the group at night. I did not have small children with me or I could not have kept this pace. In Germany, we flooded the town with flyers in the daytime and had classes at night. I also taught several group ladies' classes. In England, my husband and I spent most of our time in counseling sessions trying to help save the marriage of one of the missionary couples.

Priscilla is a Bible example of a woman who traveled with her husband and Paul. They were mentioned at several cities including Corinth, Ephesus, and Rome. Paul says both Priscilla and Aquila were fellow workers and that they risked their lives for him: "Paul stayed on in Corinth for some time. Then he left the brothers and sailed for Syria, accompanied by Priscilla and Aquila. Before he sailed, he had his hair cut off at Cenchrea because of a vow he had taken. They arrived at Ephesus, where Paul left Priscilla and Aquila" (Acts 18:18,19). Paul also said the church met in their house: "Greet Priscilla and Aquila, my fellow workers in Christ Jesus. They risked their lives for me. Not only I but all the churches of the Gentiles are grateful to them. Greet also the church that meets at their house" (Acts 16:3,4).

Mission work, whether as a promoter at home or in the field, is an exciting ministry to consider. It takes you places you never dreamed of going. I can't describe to you how I felt walking through Red Square.

Women in Literary Ministries

In years past, I enjoyed writing articles for publication in brotherhood magazines such as "Christian Family" and "Christian Woman." I've written for and edited a small magazine from our church called "Agapa." I've taken creative writing classes at a local college just because I enjoyed them. And, although I've never taken the time to really pursue a writing career, I do consider writing one of the ministries I enjoy. I think the interest started when I was a young child. My mother shared with me her interest in writing.

The primary reason I chose to put together this book is because I could not find a similar one to use in the women's ministry at the church where I attend. I had searched each bookstore I came in contact with. I asked a clerk in one Christian bookstore if she had anything on women's ministries. I told her I could not find the type of book that I felt would help the women know where they fit into the church. Before I could get the words out of my mouth, she told me it was because the Bible says men are to be the ministers, men are to lead, men are to do this and that and on and on she went. When I could get a word in, I told her that I understand what the Scriptures say and that I am in complete agreement with them, but that women are called to many ministries also. I gave her a few examples. She said, "Well, you've got it, you don't need a book." That is when I decided to finish this book, which was started years ago. I was prompted by a need I perceived wasn't being met. Maybe you feel the same way. Are there women's or children's books that you would like to write? Do you see needs in this area?

Other literary ministries include putting together lessons and visuals for children in the Bible class department at your church. The brotherhood has great material available, but sometimes to be good stewards of our money, we use our own material. This also helps us develop our literary talents.

Some women write for the pure enjoyment of writing. They write little inspirational poems and articles to be used here and there for God's glory. My friend Fern Miller is one such woman.

Literary talents may be used to write articles and news for publications such as the church bulletins, or for reporting upcoming events and items of interest to the city newspaper.

Women can teach through their own inspirational letters to another woman. Such was the case with my friend whose sister lived in Washington. Through correspondence, she aroused her sister's interest in Jesus Christ. Her sister began to study the Word and she became a Christian. She died a few months later, saved instead of lost.

This may be a ministry that you have interest in, but you have never told anyone. Well, now is the time to step out of that shell. Share your feelings and thoughts with your sisters. You'll be glad you did.

Women in Music Ministries

My friend Deb Pope can sing beautifully. She is called upon to sing at weddings, funerals, banquets, and special services. Another woman in our church has helped organize and direct a children's program of music. What an outreach this was with parents, grandparents, aunts, and uncles coming to hear their little ones sing. Women teach songs to the children in Bible class. Women sing at the nursing home. Many of you know Denise Sweet, with the singing group "Revival." Denise organized a group and, along with her husband, takes that group on the road. She is the lead singer and writes many of the songs the group sings.

This ministry is one that I have always admired. But I have to sadly admit it is not mine. God did not give me special talents in this area. Oh, I sang in high school and I love singing in church. I also played the piano and the saxophone in high school, but it did not come easy. I had no natural talents. Everything I did had to be learned by hard work and then it was only mediocre. But there are many women who have great musical talents and have made music their ministry. Their God-given talents are being used to reach out to a lost world with the message of Christ and His love. I enjoy their music and applaud them and say, "Isn't it great that God gave us different talents to be used in our ministries?"

Wives of Church Leaders—A Ministry

The wife of a preacher, an elder, or a youth minister sometimes feels her husband's ministry is also her ministry. Being a church leader's wife myself, I know this is true. I have known wives of church leaders who were not involved in their husband's ministry, and I have known wives who were heavily involved. My husband has served as an elder, preacher, and now an instructor and I have always been his co-worker. From my experience, I have observed that a preacher is much more effective if his wife is involved in the work also. A preacher's or an elder's wife may make visits with her husband to new members, visitors to the assembly, and the sick. She goes on Bible studies with him if they are studying with a couple, or a woman. She opens her home for church-related meetings of all kinds. She helps with many functions at the church. She teaches Sunday school. She is an active soul winner. Of course, this is a ministry and a very important one. She incorporates many ministries under her preacher's or elder's wife title, including the ministries of teaching, hospitality, and benevolence. Because her position demands that she be involved in many ministries, she may not be as consistent in some of them as another woman who claims only one or two ministries.

The youth minister's wife is much the same. The youth minister depends on his wife to help him work with the girls in the group, often dividing the group for the boys to meet with him and the girls with his wife. She is their counselor and teacher. The teens feel comfortable with this because they can talk more openly. The wife opens her home for youth meetings and accompanies her husband and the group on many outings and activities. This is her ministry.

Mother's Day Out Ministry

This program is usually run by women of the church as an outreach to the community and as a help to the women of the congregation. The church facility and volunteers from the church are used. You will need a director, preferably one with experience in education. Some states will require that the director have a degree. However, this is usually not the case if your Mother's Day Out program involves only one day a week, or a half-day. Call your Department of Human Services to find out what the rules are in your state.

The director will advertise the program in the church and community and the children will be enrolled prior to the first day. This is important so that the director will know how many volunteers are needed. The day should involve more than just babysitting. A curriculum should be planned involving stories, activities, playtime, lunch if applicable, snacks, and rest time if it is a complete day. If the day is open to babies, you must have cribs and seats. Usually the church's nursery is supplied with these items. You may ask each mother to bring supplies for her child in a diaper bag to cut down on additional expenses. You also may ask the mothers to bring the designated snacks such as apples or cookies.

A small fee may be charged in order to have funds for expenses and to treat your volunteers to something special from time to time.

This is a great outreach to your community. Often women who bring their children to the Mother's Day Out program start attending that church.

Newspaper Ministry

These women buy the newspaper every week and send a card in the church's name to those who have become engaged, were married, had a baby, lost a family member, or have been honored in some way. This is a great outreach for the church. It is a good-will, personal-relationship ministry.

Beautification Ministry

These are the women who keep the bulletin boards in the foyer up to date. A woman in this ministry helps the teachers with the appearance of their classrooms. She keeps flowers in the front of the auditorium, changing them as the seasons come and go. She adds special touches to the ladies' room and ladies' classroom. How are these sweet women evangelistic in this ministry? I don't know. But I bet they find ways.

Serving Ministries

The women in this ministry are those who are always serving others. They are the first to volunteer for kitchen duty for a potluck or funeral meal. They come early and stay late. They greet with a smile and a hug. The coffee is always on. How can they be evangelistic in this ministry? There is always a visitor or a newcomer in the group who needs someone to reach out to them with the love of the Lord.

These women also keep the kitchen linens and the baptismal towels and garments laundered. They prepare communion. They work in the nursery. They are always looking for ways to serve.

Professional Women's Ministry

Many times ladies' Bible classes are in the day hours and working women can't participate. For this reason they sometimes feel left out of the mainstream of things. One church corrected this problem by having all the working women meet for lunch one day a week in a private room at a local restaurant. The women ate, prayed, came together in fellowship, and had a short program that kept them in the Word. Some churches have a ladies' Bible class once a week at night for working women. It may be that your ministry is to organize this program.

Welcoming Ministry

This group of women meets once a week to work on baskets to take to new members of their congregation, especially those who have moved into the city. If their city is small, they take baskets to anyone who moves into the city, and they do not limit it to the church. In the basket, they put information about the church: times for Bible study, types of classes and programs offered, details about the staff members, the youth group, etc. They sometimes put in information about the city as well. This information can be obtained from the Chamber of Commerce. The finishing touch is homemade bread, muffins, or cookies. This ministry opens many doors for the church.

Discussion Questions

1. Could you get excited about missions? Explain.

2. Name a woman in the Bible who traveled with her husband doing mission work. Where did they travel? What did they do?

3. Do you have a secret desire to write? What types of material would you write?

4. Name ways you may use literary talents.

5. Do you have musical talents? How are you using them?

6. Discuss church leaders' wives having a ministry within their position.

7. How may a Mother's Day Out program be an outreach for your church?

8. Discuss a beautification ministry.

9. Discuss a professional women's ministry.

10. Discuss the remaining ministries.

CHAPTER THIRTEEN

It's Time for Women to Decide

We've taken a look at evangelistic women in the Bible, our power source, and the things that hinder us from being effective. We've discussed the many ministries for women. Now comes the hard part, but it's also the fun part. It's time to decide.

You may be feeling a bit overwhelmed at this point, especially if you have not been very involved in the Lord's work in the past, and now you have chosen a ministry that you know is a little out of your comfort zone. This is a normal feeling. Any change brings some uneasiness. You may want to start slowly, dabble your toes in the water to test it out. But don't hold back for long. Be ready to jump in with both feet and give it all you've got for the Lord. You will be surprised at what He will do through you.

God does not ask us to do what He doesn't give us power to do. As you get fully involved in your ministry, God will show you what He can do through you: "Test me in this, says the Lord Almighty, and see if I will not throw open the floodgates of heaven and pour out so much blessing that you will not have room enough for it" (Malachi 3:10). Again, he says, "And God is able to make all grace abound to you, so that in all things at all times, having all that you need, you will abound in every good work" (2 Cor. 9:8). And in Philippians, "I can do everything through him who gives me strength" (Phil. 4:13).

At this point, you will find many reasons why you cannot or will not acknowledge your ministry. Following are three of the most-used reasons:

1. It will get me out of my comfort zone. It will make me anxious and stressed. I will have to get out of my chair and be involved. I will have to give up my television time. I'll do some things here and there, but I don't want to obligate myself, or to be accountable to anyone.

You are like the man who hid his talent in the ground. The master was very displeased. "His master replied, 'You wicked lazy servant! So you knew that I harvest where I have not sown and gather where I have not scattered seed? Well then, you should have put my money on deposit with the bankers, so that when I returned I would have received it back with interest. Take the talent from him and give it to the one who has the ten talents'" (Matt. 25:26,2).

2. People may criticize me if I fail.

Yes, you may face criticism. You may hear things like, "You can't do that," "You've never done that before," "Why is she doing it like that," and "That's not the way we usually do it." Remember, everyone faces criticism; even those who do nothing are criticized for their lack of action. You can't control other people. Do not be concerned with them. Stick with the women who are in your ministry group who are encouraging and praying for you. Some of the people who have accomplished the greatest tasks in life were criticized in the beginning. Paul said, "Now it is required that those who have been given a trust must prove faithful. I care very little if I am judged by you or by any human court; indeed, I do not even judge myself" (1 Cor. 4:2,3).

3. I am afraid.

Do you think Jesus was afraid when He fell with his face to the ground in the garden of Gethsemane? He was overwhelmed with sorrow at what he was facing. His friends did not understand. They could not even stay awake and hold His hand. Do you think He was afraid when He was stripped, beaten, spit upon, and then led away to be crucified carrying His own cross? And was He afraid when He cried out, "My God, my God, why have you forsaken me?" I think so!

Darrel Anderson tells a story illustrating how God takes our most simple little talents, surrounds us with His power and love, and supplements and augments until a work of amazing beauty is created. Here is the story:

> The folklore surrounding Poland's famous concert pianist and prime minister, Ignace Paderewski, includes this story:
>
> A mother, wishing to encourage her young son's progress at the piano, bought tickets for a Paderewski performance. When the night arrived, they found their seats near the front of the concert hall and eyed the majestic Steinway waiting on stage. Soon the mother found a friend to talk to, and the boy slipped away. When eight o'clock arrived, the spotlights came on, the audience quieted, and only then did they notice the boy up on the bench innocently picking out "Twinkle,

Twinkle, Little Star." His mother gasped, but before she could retrieve her son, the master appeared on the stage and quickly moved to the keyboard. "Don't quit–keep playing," he whispered to the boy. Leaning over, Paderewski reached down with his left hand and began filling in a bass part. Soon his right arm reached around the other side, encircling the child, to add a running obligato. Together, the old master and the young novice held the crowd mesmerized. In our lives, unpolished though we may be, it is the Master who surrounds us and whispers in our ear, time and again, "Don't quit–keep playing." And as we do, He augments and supplements until a work of amazing beauty is created (*Teenage Christian Magazine*).

Let's put excuses aside and go forward with joy because we can serve the Lord in our ministries. Pray often with your group. It is a wonderful feeling to realize you are doing something not on your own power but on God's. You will know it is the answer to prayer. Visualize yourself being effective and talk positively to yourself. Remove all negative talk and thoughts from your mind. Shad Helmstetter's book, *What To Say When You Talk To Your Self,* tells us you become what you say and think. Our subconscious picks up on our negativity. We must program our mind with positive things. We must see ourselves interacting with other women—loving, sharing, and bringing people to the Lord.

The following are comments from women who have been involved in women's ministries:

1. "I love the planning stages of the ministry as we went through the lessons and discussed the ministries."

2. "When I read what hinders my ministry, I knew it was time to get right with God or else I would never be effective in any ministry."
3. "I like the phrase, 'I am not an ordinary woman.' That makes me feel special."
4. "I started using my talents and God blessed me with more. It is unbelievable what He can do."
5. "Serving on a committee with other women has helped to build stronger relationships with my sisters."
6. "For the first time I feel a part of the church because someone helped me fit in."
7. "I've seen the younger women develop in leadership skills."
8. "I love having a ministry."
9. "I like to be accountable. Otherwise I keep saying 'someday.'"
10. "The fellowship is just the greatest."

It is my prayer that you find great joy in serving in your ministry. In Philippians, Paul writes about many things that bring him joy, and all of them had to do with the church that he loved so dearly. He found joy in their response to the gospel, in the fact that Christ was being preached, in their faith, in Christ, in being like-minded with the brethren, in his converts who were his joy and crown, and in their concern for him. Paul uses an Old Testament example of a drink offering sacrifice: "But even if I am being poured out like a drink-offering on the sacrifice and service coming from your faith, I am glad and rejoice with all of you" (Phil. 2:17). He was willing to die as a sacrifice for Christ—

martyred because he had preached the Gospel to the Gentiles—if it would be an encouragement to the Gentiles' faith. He would even rejoice in death if it would help the cause of Christ. Your ministry probably will not cause you to be sacrificed or killed. At least not at this time in America's history. But it will cause the boundaries of the kingdom to be broadened, and it will bring you and the people around you much joy.

The early church grew rapidly because the disciples were serious about their ministries. If, among Christians today, we can create the atmosphere they had, we too will grow rapidly. We must be together, work together, and be a family of God's people.

"They devoted themselves to the apostles' teaching and to the fellowship, to the breaking of bread and to prayer. Everyone was filled with awe, and many wonders and miracles were done by the apostles. All the believers were together and had everything in common. Selling their possessions and goods they gave to anyone as he had need. Every day they continued to meet together in the temple courts. They broke bread in their homes and ate together with glad and sincere hearts, praising God and enjoying the favor of all the people. And the Lord added to their number daily those who were being saved" (Acts 2:42-47).

These early Christians said, "We cannot help speaking about what we have seen and heard" (Acts 4:20).

If there is no women's ministry in your church and no interest in starting one, you must find your ministry on your own. Look for a place where you can serve effectively. Talk to your elders about your desire to serve. God will send to you other women interested in finding their ministry. You may find yourself in the position of leader.

Discussion Questions

1. Are you ready for ministry? If not, why not?

2. Can you name your ministry or ministries in the church?

3. Are you dependable and consistent in your ministry?

4. Is your ministry evangelistic?

5. Have you acknowledged your ministry to yourself and your sisters and elders?

6. Can you name a woman in the Bible who had a similar ministry?

7. What Scriptures support your ministry?

8. How can you improve your ministry?

9. Is there a ministry that you know you have the talent to do but just don't want to take the time?

10. Discuss the story of the old master and the young novice. How does God work with us in this way?

To Help You Decide

We sometimes fill this page out in the beginning and add to it as we go through the lessons.

Name _____ Date _____

Address_____

City_____ State _____ Zip _____

Phone _____

Interests _____
_____
_____

Talents _____
_____
_____

Hobbies _____
_____
_____

Strengths _____
_____
_____

Age group you like to teach, or help teach. _____
_____

To Help You Decide

List all positive remarks you hear about yourself in class.

_____

_____

_____

_____

_____

_____

_____

_____

_____

_____

_____

_____

_____

_____

_____

_____

_____

_____

_____

_____

_____

_____

_____

It's Time to Decide

After reading and discussing each ministry, it's time to decide where you can best serve. Place a check before each ministry that you desire to develop. Discuss your choices with your Christian sisters, acknowledge them to your eldership, and have a great time serving in the kingdom.

_____ Family Ministry

_____ Hospitality Ministry

_____ Personal Teaching Ministry

_____ Ministry of Teaching Children

_____ Benevolent Ministry

_____ Counseling Ministry

_____ Encouraging Ministry

_____ Ministry with the Aging

_____ Organizational Ministry

_____ Missions Ministry

_____ Literary Ministry

_____ Music Ministry

_____ Wives of Church Leaders—A Ministry

_____ Mother's Day Out Program—A Ministry

_____ Newspaper Ministry

_____ Beautification Ministry

_____ Serving Ministry

_____ Professional Women's Ministry

_____ Welcoming Ministry

CHAPTER FOURTEEN

Guidelines for a Women's Ministry

The purpose of a women's ministry:

- To glorify God.
- To help women analyze their talents and interests.
- To help women identify and acknowledge their ministry or ministries.
- To help women work with others who have the same interests.
- To encourage each other as we serve the Lord.
- To be organized in order for women's work to be done more effectively. No more wondering if someone took care of it.

1.   If you are reading this book alone, I pray it will be helpful in determining your ministry in the church. It is not necessary to have an organized women's ministry for you to determine your ministry. On your own, or with a few friends, you can analyze your talents and decide in which ministry you have the most interest. You can become very effective and dependable and can be a great worker for the Lord.

2.   To get the most from this book it is necessary to read and study it with other women in a Bible class setting. You can start by sharing this book, and others like it, with the ladies' group at your church. They may decide to study this material in the time allotted for ladies' Bible class. This could be a Sunday morning, Sunday night, Wednesday night, or a mid-week daytime class. If the existing classes are not interested, you may want to form a small study group in your home and invite women to study this material with you. Because of the busy schedules of today's women, it is better if you can use the time already designated for Bible study.

3.   If the women already meeting for Bible study are interested, the group will need a leader. This woman may be the present teacher, the preacher's wife, or any Christian woman who is capable of leading the class and working with other women. Consider the following qualifications:

- She must be spiritually strong and mature.

- She must be loving, caring, sensitive, and compassionate.

- She must have good leadership skills.

- She must be able to organize and motivate.

- She must have the necessary time to work with the women in the group.

4.   The leader should ask for the approval of the elders or the leadership of the congregation. A women's ministry works under the leadership of the church. It should never work against the leadership. It must be in tune with the church. These things should be brought before the elders:

- Tell them what the class is about and what you expect to gain from the class.

- Show them the material you plan to cover.

- Ask permission to meet with the educational director to schedule this class when the current Bible study has ended.

- Ask for a list of works they would like the women to do, or supply them with a list for their approval. If they are not interested in an organized women's ministry, go back to step one.

5.   Start with prayer before every class. It is God who gives each of us talents, and without Him we can do nothing. Talk to Him about the women's desire to learn to be the best servants possible. Ask Him to lead each woman to the ministry in which she can be the most effective.

6.   Study one lesson each week until you have covered all the lessons. Make your classes comfortable and informal. Sit in a circle if the class is small enough. You may choose to serve coffee or tea to create an

atmosphere much like sitting around your table at home.

7. Before the first lesson, each woman should fill out the "To Help You Decide" pages. This may be difficult for some, because they have not yet studied the ministries. Others will change their mind during the course of the studies.

8. Pay close attention to the lessons on "Evangelistic Women," "Power For Effective Ministries," and "What Hinders My Ministry" before discussing the ministries. Some women in the group will not be prepared for ministry until they have studied these lessons. Provide an atmosphere for women to share openly, and ask for help in areas of need.

9. After each lesson, divide the class into small groups of three or four women for discussion. Each woman should share her feelings about the ministry discussed in the lesson and how it may or may not apply to her. She is not making a decision at this time, only brainstorming with the group.

10. Periodically have entire class brainstorming discussions. Have everyone sit in a circle and ask each to share her talents and interests and how she feels she can use them in the church. Go around the circle and have the other women comment on what they perceive to be the talents of the woman who is sharing. She should write all positive comments that she hears from her classmates on her "To Help You Decide" pages. These comments will help her later in her decision.

11. At least twice during the course, have a session where each woman shares positive attributes about the woman to her right. When she has finished, allow other members of the group to affirm if they choose. These sharing sessions are very important. Each woman needs to hear positive comments from her classmates.

As she listens to what other women see as her talents and strong points, it will help her determine her ministry. Have each woman write all positive comments about herself on the "To Help You Decide" pages. Have several sharing sessions during the course of the studies.

12. Periodically have an intense prayer session. You can't pray too much when you are studying something this important.

13. After the last lesson each woman should:

- Consider the positive remarks she has heard from other women concerning her strong points and talents.

- Examine her talents and interests.

- Consider what she is often asked to do.

- Look over the ministries discussed.

- Ask God to bless her in making the right decision.

- Fill out the "It's Time to Decide" sheet.

- Acknowledge her decision to her classmates and the elders of the congregation.

- Look for an opportunity to serve in the desired ministry.

This time each woman is making a decision to work in a particular area. This decision can be changed, if she later decides she is better suited for another area of work. Each woman should identify her ministries and acknowledge them to the class. She should be as detailed as possible. She should not compare herself with anyone else. Everyone has different talents and interests.

14. The leader should help each woman identify and acknowledge her ministry even if she has to meet with her outside of class for a personal session. No one should finish the class saying they do not have a ministry unless they do not have a heart to serve the Lord.

15. Present these decisions to the elders so they may know the success of the class and the areas the women will be developing their talents.

16. When the class is completed, it is important that the leader call the group together once a month for encouragement and support. At this meeting there should be encouragement from the Scriptures and much discussion among the women as to how they are doing. They will discuss what is working and what is not. What are their needs? What could make their ministries more effective? Some will want to ask advice of the group. Some will share success stories.

17. The leader may want to divide the group into subgroups for expanding and learning about certain ministries. For example, all the women who want to learn to lead a personal Bible study with someone who is not a Christian will want to meet together to discuss the lessons they plan to teach and how to make contacts for new studies. All the women who are going to write cards and notes will want to organize in order to be more effective. Sub-leaders will emerge also. This will help the women who have leadership talents to develop them. Remember, each ministry should be evangelistic, if at all possible. These meetings should not take the place of the once-a-month meeting for the whole group.

18. The women's ministry leader should meet with the sub-leaders periodically to help keep everything running smoothly and to help these women grow as leaders. It is possible that some have never served as leaders, and they will need help. The leader is not there to boss them around, but to help them grow and to know what is going on in all the groups in order to account to the elders.

19. The leader should type a list of all ministries and those participating in each one to give to the elders and to distribute to new women coming into the congregation. The leader should also periodically hold a class for new women to help them identify their ministries and to direct them to other women with similar ministries.

20. As women begin their new ministries, everyone must remember to be complimentary. We must be observant and attentive. A word of encouragement goes a long way for a woman who is starting something she hasn't done before.

A women's ministry may not be effective if the elders do not want an organized women's group, or if the work of the church is already being done effectively through care groups or shepherding groups. If this is the case, let your shepherd or care group leader know the outcome of your study, and ask for a place to use your ministry in the group.

God will do great things through you and your women's ministry groups. Please write me with your success stories. I will share them with the women in my classes at the Bear Valley Bible Institute. It will give them courage to help the women in their future congregations to find their ministries.

What Is a Ministry?

It is a ministry:

If God is glorified.
If you are consistent, dependable, and accountable.
If you continue even when no one notices.
If it costs your time, energy, thoughts, and sometimes your money.
If you are excited about the results.
If you continue to serve when you are criticized.
If souls are being saved.
If you are daily asking God for help.

It is not a ministry:

If you only do it when you feel like it.
If you are doing it to seek the praise of others.
If it costs you nothing.
If you are not excited about serving the Lord.
If you quit when someone criticizes you.
If you are not concerned about souls.
If you are not praying about it.

Discussion Questions

1. What is the purpose of a women's ministry?

2. Discuss how to approach the elders concerning a women's ministry.

3. What do you do if the elders do not want an organized women's ministry in the church?

4. Discuss qualifications for a women's ministry leader.

5. Discuss the advantages of small group discussions.

6. Discuss the advantages of talking about your talents and interests to your classmates, and the advantages of hearing their comments.

7. Discuss the advantages of affirming one another.

8. Discuss the purpose of meeting together once a month after the class is completed.

9. Why is it important for each woman to make a decision concerning her ministry?

10. How will you get new members involved in the women's ministry?

Name _____

What is my ministry in the church?

_____

_____

Am I evangelistic in my ministry?

_____

_____

Have I acknowledged my ministry to myself, my sisters, and my elders?

_____

_____

Am I dependable and consistent in my ministry?

_____

_____

Is there a woman in the Bible that I can name who had a similar ministry?

_____

_____

How can I improve my ministry?

_____

_____

CHAPTER FIFTEEN

Bible Women

Old Testament Women

Abigail	1 Samuel 25:3; 2 Samuel 3:3
Abigail no. 2	2 Samuel 17:25; 1 Chronicles 2:16,17
Abihail	Numbers 3:35
Abihail no. 2	1 Chronicles 2:29
Abihail no. 3	2 Chronicles 11:18
Abijah	2 Kings 18:2; 2 Chronicles 29:1
Abijah no. 2	1 Chronicles 2:24
Abishag	1 Kings 1:3,4; 2:13-25
Achsah	Joshua 15:16,17; Judges 1:12,13
Adah	Genesis 4:19-23
Adah no. 2	Genesis 36:2
Ahinoam	1 Samuel 14:50
Ahinoam no. 2	1 Samuel 25:43; 27:3; 30:5;
	2 Samuel 2:2; 3:2; 1 Chronicles 3:1
Ahlai	1 Chonricles 2:31,34
Ahlai no. 2	1 Chronicles 11:41
Aholibamah	Genesis 36:2-25

Anah	Genesis 36:2,18,25
Asenath	Genesis 41:45-50
Atarah	1 Chronicles 2:26
Athaliah	2 Kings 8:26;
	2 Chronicles 22:3; 23:12,13,21; 24:7
Azubah	1 Chronicles 2:18-19
Azubah no. 2	1 Kings 22:42; 2 Chronicles 20:31
Baara	1 Chronicles 8:8
Bashemath	Genesis 26:34; 36:10
Bashemath no. 2	1 Kings 4:15
Bathsheba	2 Samuel 11:2,3; 12;24;
	1 Kings 1:11-31; 2:13-19;
	1 Chronicles 3:5
Bilhah	Genesis 29:29; 30:3-5; 35:22; 37:2;
	46:25
Bithiah	1 Chronicles 4:18
Cozbi	Numbers 25:6-15
Deborah	Genesis 35:8
Deborah no. 2	Judges 4 and 5
Delilah	Judges 16:4-21
Dinah	Genesis 34
Eglah	2 Samuel 3:5; 1 Chronicles 3:3
Elisheba	Exodus 6:23
Ephah	1 Chronicles 2:46
Ephrath	1 Chronicles 2:19,50
Esther	The Book of Esther
Eve	Genesis 2 and 3; 2 Corinthians 11:3;
	1 Timothy 2:13
Gomer	Hosea 1:3
Hagar	Genesis 16; 21:9-17; 25:12;
	Galatians 4:24,25
Haggith	2 Samuel 3:4,5; 1 Kings 1:5,11; 2:13;
	1 Chronicles 3:2
Hammoleketh	1 Chronicles 7:17,18
Hamutal	Jeremiah 52:1,2; 2 Kings 23:31; 24:18

Hannah	1 Samuel 1:1-10,21
Hazelelponi	1 Chronicles 4:3
Helah	1 Chronicles 4:5,7
Hephzibah	2 Kings 21:1
Hodesh	1 Chronicles 8:8-9
Hodiah	1 Chronicles 4:18,19; Nehemiah 10:18
Hoglah	Numbers 26:33; 27:1-11; 36:1-12; Joshua 17:3
Huldah	2 Kings 22:14-20; 2 Chronicles 34:22-33
Hushim	1 Chronicles 8:8,11
Iscah	Genesis 11:29
Jael	Judges 4:17-22; 5:6,24-27
Jecoliah	2 Kings 15:2
Jedidah	2 Kings 22:1,2
Jehoaddan	2 Kings 14:2
Jehosheba	2 Kings 11:2
Jemima	Job 42:14
Jerioth	1 Chronicles 2:18
Jerusha	2 Kings 15:33; 2 Chronicles 27:1-6
Jezebel	1 Kings 16:31; 18:4-19; 19:1,2; 21:5-25; 2 Kings 9:29-37
Jochebed	Numbers 26:59
Judith	Genesis 26:34
Keren-Happuch	Job 42:14
Keturah	Genesis 25:1-6; 1 Chronicles 1:32,33
Kezia	Job 42:14
Leah	Genesis 29:16-35
Lo-ruhamah	Hosea 1:6-8
Maachah	1 Chronicles 2:48; 7:12,15,16
Mara	Ruth 1:20
Matred	Genesis 36:39
Mehetabel	Genesis 36:39; 1 Chronicles 1:50
Merab	1 Samuel 14:49; 18:17,19

Meshullemeth	2 Kings 21:19
Michal	1 Samuel 14:49; 18:20-28; 19:11-17; 25:44; 2 Samuel 3:13,14; 6:16-23; 1 Chronicles 15:29
Milcah	Genesis 22:20,23; 24:15,24,47
Milcah no. 2	Numbers 26:33; 27:1; 36:11; Joshua 17:3
Miriam	Exodus 15:20,21; Numbers 12:1-15; 20-1; 26:59; Dueteronomy 23:9; Micah 6:4
Miriam no. 2	1 Chronicles 4:17
Naamah	Genesis 4:22
Naamah no. 2	1 Kings 14:21,31; 2 Chronicles 12:13
Naarah	1 Chronicles 4:5,6
Naomi	The Book of Ruth
Nehushta	2 Kings 24:8
Noah	Numbers 26:33; 27:1
Orpah	Ruth 1
Peninnah	1 Samuel 1:2
Puah	Exodus 1:15
Rachel	Genesis 29; 30; 31; 33:1,2,7; 35:16-26; 46:19,22,25; 48:7; Ruth 4:11; 1 Samuel 10:2
Rahab	Joshua 6:17-25; Matthew 1:5; Hebrews 11:31; James 2:25
Rebekah	Genesis 22:23; 24; 25:20-28; 26:6-35; 27; 28:5; 29:12; 35:8; 49:31 Romans 9:6-16
Reumah	Genesis 22:24
Rizpah	2 Samuel 3:7; 21:8-14
Ruth	The Book of Ruth; Matthew 1:5
Sarai	Genesis 11:29-31; 12:5-17; 16:1-8; 17:15-21; 18; 20:2-18; 21:1-12; 23:1-19; 24:36,37; 25:10,12; 49:31; Isaiah 51:2; Romans 4:19; 9:9; Hebrews 11:11; 1 Peter 3:6

Serah	Genesis 46:17; 1 Chronicles 7:30
Shelomith	Leviticus 24:10-13
Shelomith no. 2	1 Chronicles 3:19
Sheerah	1 Chronicles 7:24
Shimeath	2 Kings 12:21; 2 Chronicles 24:26
Shiphrah	Exodus 1:15
Shomer	2 Kings 12:21
Shua	Genesis 38:1,2; 1 Chronicles 7:32
Tahpenes	1 Kings 11:19,20
Tamar	Genesis 38:6-30; Ruth 4:12; 1 Chronicles 2:4; Matthew 1:3
Tamar no. 2	2 Samuel 13; 1 Chronicles 3:9
Tamar no. 3	2 Samuel 14:27
Taphath	1 Kings 4:11
Timna	Genesis 36:12,22; 1 Chronicles 1:39
Tirzah	Numbers 26:33
Vashti	Esther 1; 2:1
Zebidah	2 Kings 23:36
Zeresh	Esther 5:10,14; 6:13
Zeruiah	2 Samuel 17:25; 1 Chronicles 2:16
Zibiah	2 Kings 12:1; 2 Chronicles 24:1
Zillah	Genesis 4:19-23
Zilpah	Genesis 29:24; 30:9,10; 35:26; 37:2; 46:18
Zipporah	Exodus 2:21,22; 4:24,25; 18:1-6

New Testament Women

Anna   Luke 2:36-38

Phrophetess, widow, was old in years, worshipped night and day at the temple, witnessed Jesus at the temple, spoke about Jesus to all who would listen.

Apphia   Philemon 2

Greeted by Paul in the Philemon letter. She is called "our sister."

Bernice   Acts 25:13,23; 26:30
The wife of King Agrippa. Festus asked Agrippa to hear Paul's case. Bernice came with Agrippa. They found nothing in Paul that deserved death or imprisonment.

Candace   Acts 8:27
Queen of Ethiopia, The Ethiopian church was an important official in charge of all her treasury. History says that the eunuch was able to teach her about Jesus.

Chloe   1 Corinthians 1:11
Some from her household had informed Paul of quarrels among them. This indicates that possibly the church met at her house.

Claudia   2 Timothy 4:21
Mentioned with those who sent greetings to Timothy. From this we assume she was a faithful worker with Paul.

Damaris   Acts 17:34
A believer, a follower of Paul.

Dorcas   Acts 9:36-43
Also called Tabitha. Made robes and other clothes for the poor. She died and Peter raised her from the dead.

Drusilla   Acts 24:24
Wife of Felix. Came with her husband to listen to Paul speak about Jesus.

Elizabeth   Luke 1:5-66
Mother of John the Baptist. Relative of Mary, Jesus' mother.

Eunice   Acts 16:1-3; 2 Timothy 1:5; 3:14,15; 4:5
Mother of Timothy. Raised a godly son.

Euodia   Philippians 4:2
Worked at Paul's side in the cause of the gospel. One of the women at Philippi who was involved in a conflict.

Eve   2 Corinthians 11:3; 1 Timothy 2:13
Old Testament woman also mentioned in the New Testament. The first woman.

Hagar   Galatians 4:24-25
Old Testament woman referred to in the New Testament.

Herodias   Matthew 14:3-12; Mark 6:14-24;
                    Luke 3:19,20
Herod's brother Philip's wife.

Jezebel   Revelations 2:18-29
A figurative woman. Not a real woman.

Joanna   Luke 8:1-3; 24:10
Manager of Herod's household. Cured of evil spirits and demons. Wife of Cuza. Helped support Jesus and the disciples out of her own means. Was among the women who witnessed Jesus' death, prepared spices and ointments for his body, gathered with others at the tomb the next day. Beheld the angels and heard them say that Jesus had risen. Was listed with the women who were the first to proclaim that Jesus was risen.

Julia   Romans 16:15
Paul sent greetings to her in the Roman letter. She must have been a prominent member of the church.

Lois   2 Timothy 1:5
Timothy's grandmother who helped raise him up to
be a godly son.

Lydia   Acts 16:12-15,40; Philippians 1:1-10
A business woman, a dealer in purple. She was the
first convert at Philippi.

Martha   Luke 10:38-41; John 11:17-34; 12:1-3
Sister of Mary. Great at serving.

Mary   Luke 10:38-41; John 11:17-34; 12:1-3
Sister of Martha. Sat at Jesus' feet to learn. Poured
perfume on Jesus' feet and wiped his feet with her
hair.

Mary   Matthew 1:16; 18-25; Luke 1:26-56;
                        John 2:1-11; Acts 1:14
Chosen by God to give birth to His Son.

Mary Magdalene   Matthew 27:55-61; 28:1-10;
                        Mark 15:40-47; 16:1-13;
                        Luke 8:2; 24:10; John 19:25; 20:1-18
Healed of evil spirits by Jesus. Helped Jesus and the
disciples out of her own means. Was among the
people who followed Jesus on His last journey to the
cross, was at his burial, beheld the angels at the
tomb, and Jesus appeared to her first when he had
risen. She was one of the first to have the privilege
of announcing that Jesus had risen.

Mary   Matthew 27:55-61; Mark 15:40,47;
                        16:1; Luke 24:10
Mother of James and Joses. Was with the women
watching from afar when Jesus was crucified.

Mary   Acts 12:12
Mother of John Mark. Christians met at her house for prayer. Peter went there when he escaped from prison. Raised a godly man.

Mary of Rome   Romans 16:6
Paul greets her in the Roman letter.

Persis   Romans 16:12
Paul's dear friend. Worked hard in the Lord.

Phoebe   Romans 16:1,2
Servant in the church in Cenchrea. Sister in the Lord.

Priscilla   Acts 18:2,18,26; Romans 16:3;
                       1 Corinthians 16:19; 2 Timothy 4:19
Fellow worker with Paul. Traveled with her husband and Paul on one of the missionary journeys. Married to Aquila. Paul stayed and worked with them at their home in Corinth.

Rhoda   Acts 12:13
Servant girl who saw Peter at the door after his escape from prison.

Salome   Mark 15:40,41; 16:1,2
Watched from a distance at the crucifixion. Helped care for Jesus' needs. Brought spices to annoint His body. Was at the tomb when the angel said He had risen. Mother of Zebedee's sons who asked Jesus if her sons could sit on His right and left in the kingdom.

Sapphira   Acts 5:1-11
Lied about money that she brought to the disciples for the work. Fell dead.

Susanna   Luke 8:2,3
Cured of evil spirits by Jesus. Listed with Mary
Magdalene, Joanna, and others as supporter of Jesus
and the apostles.

Syntyche   Philippians 4:2
Member of the church at Philippi. Worked at Paul's
side for the cause of the gospel. Had a disagreement
with Euodia.

Tryphena   Romans 16:12
Greeted by Paul in Romans. Worked very hard in
the Lord.

Tryphosa   Romans 16:12
Greeted by Paul in Romans. Worked very hard in
the Lord.

Bibliography

Anderson, Darrell, "Teenage Christian Magazine."

Bright, Vonette and Barbara Ball, *The Joy of Hospitality*, Orlando: New Life Publications, 1996.

Collins, Gary R., *How to be a People Helper*, Wheaton, IL: Tyndale House Publications, Inc., 1995.

Gifford, Michael, *The ABCs of Family Life*, Commerce, GA: Whitlise Publications, 1987.

Holloway, Dale, *12 Ways to Develop a Positive Attitude*, Wheaton, IL: Tyndale House Publishers, Inc., 1975.

Pearl, Michael and Debi Pearl, *To Train Up a Child*, Pleasantville, TN: The Church at Cane Creek Publishing, 1994.

Evangelistic Women Order Form

Use this convenient order form to order additional copies
of
Evangelistic Women

Please Print:

Name_____

Address_____

City_____ **State**_____

Zip_____

Phone(**)**_____

_____ copies of book @ $_____ each $ _____
Postage and handling @ $_____ per book $ _____
___ residents add ___% tax $ _____
Total amount enclosed $ _____

Make checks payable to Pamela Stewart

Send to BPS Publications
14069 W. Amherst Av. • Lakewood, CO 80228-5312
(303)984-9136